COLLECTED WRITINGS OF W. D. GANN

VOLUME 6

W. D. GANN'S COLLECTED ASTROLOGICAL WRITINGS & CHARTS

BY

WILLIAM D. GANN

COSMOLOGICAL ECONOMICS
WWW.COSMOECONOMICS.COM

ORIGINALLY PUBLISHED 1955

THIS SERIES IS PUBLISHED BY THE:
INSTITUTE OF COSMOLOGICAL ECONOMICS

COSMOLOGICAL ECONOMICS
IS AN IMPRINT OF:
SACRED SCIENCE INSTITUTE
WWW.SACREDSCIENCE.COM
INSTITUTE@SACREDSCIENCE.COM
US: 800-756-6141 θ INTL: 951-659-8181

COSMOLOGICAL ECONOMICS

THE MASTERS OF FINANCIAL ASTROLOGY SERIES

The Masters of Financial Astrology Series brings together a collection of the most important classical and modern works on Astroeconomics or astrological financial market forecasting. These classic works written from the Golden Age of Technical Analysis to current times were carefully selected by the late Dr. Jerome Baumring of the Investment Centre Bookstore in the 1980's, as representing the most valuable and important works in financial astrology ever written. They were included as the foundational source texts for his program in advanced financial market analysis and forecasting, and serve as the ideal foundation for any analyst seeking a thorough education in astrological applications to financial market theory and forecasting.

The Golden Age of technical analysis was a period from the early 1900's through the 1960's where the foundational theories of modern financial analysis and financial astrology came into full form. The ideas and technologies developed during this fruitful period include the first serious research into the modern field of Astro-Economics, or Financial Astrology and related fields like cycle analysis, cosmic causation, solar influence on geomagnetic and Earthly events like weather, earthquakes, climate change and radio disturbance. Though financial astrology is actually a subject that stretches back centuries, if not millennia, this ripe period saw the real advent of popular research and theoretical development of this vast study of the interaction between cosmic forces and Earthly phenomena. This collection represents the best work available within this field.

Each quality reprint of these classical texts has been reproduced as an exact facsimile of the original text, maintaining the original layout, typeset, charts, and style of the author and time period, helping to preserve and communicate a sense of the feeling of the original work that a reproduction in modern format does not capture. Many of these rare works and courses were originally printed in only very small private editions or as correspondence courses, so that the originals were easily lost or destroyed over time. Our reproductions of these important source works are printed on acid free paper and bound in a quality hardcover that will compliment any trading library and help to preserve this important resource for generations to come.

The series is also currently being digitized and archived for permanent digital preservation by the Institute of Cosmological Economics, creating a searchable reference library of market wisdom accessible globally and available in new digital formats to keep the knowledge fresh and accessible through new devices and technology as we advance further into the information revolution. To see our full catalog of hardcover reprints, new publications, and digital editions please visit our website at www.CosmoEconomics.com.

Astrological Writings And Charts

W. D. Gann

Chapter 1 — *Method For Forecasting The Stock Market*
1921 This is the only course mentioning planetary correlations with time cycles.

Chapter 2 — *The Human Body And Time Cycles*
1931 A fascinating essay on the symbolic interpretation of the human body. Discusses number symbolism, geometry, time cycles and astrology with market correlations.

Chapter 3 — *Soy Beans Price Resistance Levels, Active Angles And Degrees Of Zodiac*

Chapter 4 — *May Coffee Santos D, Heliocentric And Geocentric Aspects And Planets*

Chapter 5 — *Astrological Charts And Tables*
Mean of 5 – Cycle of 8 – Jupiter And Saturn Scale Cycles – Astrological Calculations – Heliocentric Average of 6 planets – May Coffee Moon Signs – Path of the Planets

CHAPTER 1

METHOD FOR FORECASTING THE STOCK MARKET

SCIENTIFIC ADVICE
AND ANALYTICAL REPORTS
ON STOCKS AND COMMODITIES
AUTHOR OF "TRUTH OF THE STOCK TAPE"
AND "THE TUNNEL THRU THE AIR"

W. D. GANN
78 WALL STREET
NEW YORK

MEMBER
AMERICAN ECONOMIC AS
ROYAL ECONOMIC SOCI
CABLE ADDRESS
"GANWADE NEWYORK"

METHOD FOR FORECASTING THE STOCK MARKET

KIND OF CHARTS

You should keep a yearly, monthly, weekly and overnight chart. You will find on the weekly chart that stocks will often reverse the minor trend and run up two or three weeks, but the third week it will not make a higher top or a higher bottom; yet at other times it will hold for several weeks without advancing above the level made in the first two weeks' rally. In cases of this kind, it is always safe to buy or sell with a stop 3 points above or below the two weeks' reverse move. If the market is going higher, it should continue up the third week, or down, as the case may be. The rules apply in a bear market as in a bull market.

The Overnight Chart, in order to show a reversal in trend, must go 3 points above the last top or bottom. The Overnight Chart is based on Bottoms. As long as higher bottoms are made, it continues upward. As long as lower bottoms are made, it continues downward. The basis of all movements are calculated from bottoms. For a market to advance, bottoms must be progressive or increasing, and if a market declines, bottoms must decrease.

HOW TO FORECAST

Every movement in the market is the result of a natural law and of a Cause which exists long before the Effect takes place and can be determined years in advance. The future is but a repetition of the past, as the Bible plainly states: "The thing that hath been, it is that which shall be; and that which is done is that which shall be done, and there is no new thing under the sun." -Eccl. 1:9.

Everything has a major and a minor, and in order to be accurate in forecasting the future, you must know the major cycle, as the most money is made when extreme fluctuations occur.

The major cycle of stocks occurs every 49 to 50 years. A period of "jubilee" years of extreme high or low prices, lasting from 5 to 7 years occur at the end of the 50-year cycle.

"7" is a fatal number referred to many times in the Bible and it is ruled by the planet Saturn, which brings about contractions, depression, and panics. Seven times "7" equals 49, which is shown as the fatal evil year, causing extreme fluctuations.

The most important Time cycle is the 20-year cycle, or 240 months and most stocks and averages work closer to this cycle than any other. Five years is one-quarter of twenty and ten years is one-half of twenty and very important because it is 120 months. Fifteen years is three-quarters of twenty years and important because it is 180 months, just the same as 7 1/2 years is 90 months, because 84 5/8 is 15/16 of 90.

The next important major cycle is 30 years, which is caused by the planet Saturn. This planet makes one revolution around the sun every 30 years. Saturn rules the products of the earth and causes extreme high or low prices in products of the earth at the end of each 30-year cycle, and this makes Stocks high or low. The most important cycle of all is the 20-year cycle.

The next important major cycle is the 10-year cycle, which produces fluctuations of the same nature and extreme high or low every 10 years. Stocks come out remarkably close on each even 10-year cycle. The minor cycles are 3 years and 6 years. The smallest cycle is 1 year, which will often show a change in the 10th or 11th month.

In rapid markets a move will run 6 to 7 weeks and have some kind of a minor reversal in trend, but often markets will continue for several months, only reacting two weeks, then resting possibly two or three weeks and resuming the main trend. Often they move right on up or down in the third week. This same rule applies to daily movements. Fast markets will only move two days in the opposite direction to the main trend and on the third day they will resume their upward or downward course in harmony with the main trend.

In all movements use the angles and also calculate the 1/3, 2/3, 1/4, and 3/4 points of the major or minor move. One-half is the most important as it equals the 45° angle, which is the strongest and most fatal. The next in importance is 2/3, which would equal a triangle, or 120°.

All rules based on Natural Law are applied the same to Time, Space and Volume charts.

It never pays to guess. Always consider the main time swing of a market; then watch your weekly and Overnight charts until they show a reversal or time has expired. All markets move in three to four sections. The third or fourth movement up or down marks the culmination. A reverse signal is always given before time expires and then the market may make two or three swings up or down into the same territory, going a little higher or a little lower than the tops or bottoms from which the warning signal was given. When this is taking place the market is either being accumulated or distributed.

TIME RULES FOR FORECASTING STOCKS

The stock market moves in 10-year cycles, which is worked out in 5-year cycles -- a 5-year cycle up and a 5-year cycle down.

Rule 1: Bull or bear campaigns do not run more than 3 to 3½ years up or down without a move of 3 to 6 months or one year in the opposite direction. Many campaigns culminate in the 23rd month, not running out the full two years. Watch the weekly and monthly charts to determine whether the culmination will occur in the 23rd or 24th month of the move, or in the 34 to 35, 41 to 42, 49 to 60, 67 to 72, or 84 to 90th months.

Rule 2: A Bull campaign runs five years, -2 years up, 1 year down, and 2 years up, completing a 5-year cycle. The end of a 5-year campaign comes in the 59th or 60th months. Always watch for the change in the 59th month.

Rule 3: A Bear cycle runs five years down. First move 2 years down, then 1 year up and 2 years down - completing the 5-year down swing.

Rule 4: Add ten years to any top and it will give you another top of a 10 year cycle with about the same average fluctuations.

Rule 5: Add ten years to any bottom and it will give you the next bottom of the 10-year cycle and of the same kind of a year and about the same average fluctuations.

Rule 6: Bear campaigns run out in 7-year cycles, or 3 years and 4 years from any complete bottom. From any complete bottom of a cycle first add 3 years to get the next bottom; then add 4 years to get bottom of 7-year cycle.

Rule 7: From any complete top add three years to get the next top; then add three years to the first top, which will give the second top. Add four years to the second top to get the third and final top of a 10-year cycle.

Rule 8: Add five years to any top, will give the next bottom of a five-year cycle with about the same average fluctuations. In order to get tops of a 5-year cycle, add five years to any bottom and it will give the next top with the same average fluctuations. 1917 bottom of a big bear campaign - add five years gives 1922 top of a minor bull campaign. Why do I say "Top of a Minor Bull Campaign"? 1919 was top - add five years to 1919, gives 1924 as bottom of a 5-year Bear cycle. Refer to Rule 2 and 3, which will tell you that a Bull or Bear campaign never runs more than two years in the same direction.

The Bear campaign from 1919 was down two years - 1920 and 1921: therefore, we can only get a 1-year rally in 1922; then two years down - 1923 and 1924, which completes the 5-year Bear cycle. Now, look back to 1913 and 1914 and you will see that 1923 and 1924 must be Bear years to complete the 10-year cycle from the bottoms of 1913 and 1914. Then note 1917 bottom of a Bear year. add seven years and it gives 1924 also as bottom of a Bear cycle.

Rule 9: How to make up Annual Forecasts for any year. Take ten years back and the future year will run very close to the last 10-year cycle. For instance - 1932 will run like 1902, 1912, and 1922.

There is a major cycle of 30 years, which runs out three ten-year cycles. The 10-year cycle back from the present and the 20-year cycle have the most effect on the future. But in completing the 30-year cycle, it is best to have 30 years past records to check up to make up a future forecast. For instance: In order to make up my 1922 Forecast, I check 1892, 1902, and 1912, and watch for minor variations in monthly moves. But I know that 1922 will run closest to 1912. However, some stocks will run close to the fluctuations of 1892 and 1902. Remember each stock works from its own base or from its own tops and bottoms, and not always according to Average tops and bottoms. Therefore, judge each stock individually and keep up weekly and monthly charts on them.

Rule 10: Extreme Great Cycles. There must always be a major and a minor, a lesser and a greater, a positive and a negative; that is why stocks have three important moves in a 10-year cycle, two tops three years apart and the next one four years. This works again the five years moves, 2 years up and 1 year down, then 2 years up - two major and one minor move. The smallest complete cycle or workout in a market is five years, and 10 is a complete cycle. Five times ten equals 50, which is the greatest cycle. At the end of a Great Cycle of 50 years, extreme high and low prices occur. Go back over past records and you can verify this.

The number "7" is the basis of time, and a panick occurs and depression in the stock market every seven years, which is extreme and greater than the three-year decline. Note 1907, 1917, etc. Seven times seven is fatal, which makes 49 years, and causes extreme fluctuations in the 49th to 50th year. Remember that you must begin with bottoms or tops to figure all cycles, whether major or minor. Extreme fluctuations also occur at the end of a 30-year cycle as you can see by going back 30 to 50 years.

Rule 11: Monthly moves can be determined by the same rule as yearly; i. e., add three months to a bottom, then add four, making seven, to get minor bottoms and reaction points. But remember in a Bull market a reaction may only last two or three weeks; then the advance is resumed. In this way, a market may continue up for twelve months without breaking a monthly bottom. In Big up

SWING A reaction will not last over two months, the third month being up, the same rule as in yearly cycle - two down and the third up. This same rule applies in Bear markets - rallies not lasting more than two months. Most moves run out in six to seven weeks. Seven days in a week, and seven times seven making 49 days, a fatal turning point. Always watch your annual trend and consider whether you are in a bear or Bull market. Many times when in a Bull year, with the monthly chart showing up, a stock will react two or three weeks, then rest three or four weeks, going into new territory and advancing six to seven weeks more. Always consider whether or not your big time limit has run out before judging a reverse move, and do not fail to consider your indications on time both from main tops and bottoms.

Rule 12: Daily Charts: The daily swing runs on the same rules as yearly and monthly cycles, but of course it is only a minor part of them. Important daily changes occur every seven and ten days. During a month natural changes in trend occur around the 6th to 7th, 9th to 10th, 14th to 15th, 19th to 20th, 23rd to 24th, 29th to 31st. These minor moves occur in accordance with tops and bottoms of individual stocks. Watch for a change in Trend 30 days from the last top or bottom. This is very important. Then watch for changes 60 90, 120 days from tops or bottoms. 180 days, or six months, is very important and sometimes marks changes for greater moves. Also the 9th and 11th months from tops or bottoms should be watched for important minor and often major changes.

A daily chart gives the first short change, which may run for seven or ten days, the Weekly the next important changes in trend, and the monthly the strongest. Remember weekly moves run three to seven weeks; monthly moves 2 to 3 months or more, according to the yearly cycle, before reversing.

It is important to note whether a stock is making higher or lower bottoms each year. For instance, if a stock has made a higher bottom each year for five years, then makes a lower than previous year, it is a sign of a reversal and may mark a long down cycle. The same rule applies in stocks that are making lower tops for a number of years in a Bear market.

Study all the instructions and rules I have given you. Read them over several times, as each time they will become clearer to you. Study the charts and work out the rules in actual practice, as well as on past performances. In this way you will make progress and will realize and appreciate the value of my method of forecasting.

INSTRUCTIONS FOR FORECASTING THE STOCK MARKET

First, remember time is the most important of all factors and not until sufficient time has expired does any big move up or down start. The time factor will overbalance both space and volume. When time is up, space movement will start and big volume will begin either up or down, Time rules. Always consider your annual Forecast.

Second, consider each individual stock and determine its trend from its position according to distance in time from bottom or top. Each stock works out its 5, 10, 20, 30, 50 and 60 year cycles from its own bottoms and tops, regardless of the movements of other stocks, even those in the same group.

Third, monthly reversals or changes in trend often occur after two to three months. The change starts in the third month, according to the main time factor you are working in.

Fourth, weekly time rules. A stock will run down two to three weeks and sometimes four, but as a rule a reversal or change will occur in the third week and will only run three weeks against the main trend. In a Bull market two weeks' decline, or possible three, and in the middle of the third week the trend will turn up and close higher at the end of the third week. In some cases the change in trend will not come until the fourth week. Then the reversal will come and it will close higher at the end of the fourth week. All of these rules are reversed in a bear market.

Fifth, rapid advances or declines on big volume will run about seven weeks. These are culmination moves up or down. Watch for bottom or top around the 49th to 52nd day, although at times the bottom or top will come on the 42nd to 45th day and a change in trend will start.

Remember that at the end of any big movement, either monthly, weekly, or daily move, sometime must be consumed for accumulation or distribution. So, you must allow for this. Watch your angles and time periods. After a market has declined seven weeks, it may have two or three short weeks on the side and then turn up, which agrees with the monthly rule for a change in the third month.

In regard to daily time rules, the daily chart gives the first change but remember it may only run from seven to ten days, then follow the main trend. The weekly chart will give the next important change in trend but remember it may not run more than three to four weeks or in extreme cases not more than six to seven weeks, then reverse. and follow the main trend.

The monthly chart may reverse and run down three to four months, then reverse and follow the main trend again, or run up three to four months in a bear market, then reverse and follow the main trend, although as a general rule, in a bear market stocks never rally more than two months. They start breaking in the third month and follow the main trend down.

Never decide that the main trend has changes one way or the other without consulting your angles from top or bottom and without considering the position you are in in the cycle of each individual stock. When extreme advances or declines occur, the first time that the market reverses over one-fourth or one-half of the distance traveled, in the last section, you can consider that the trend has turned up or down at least for the present.

It is important to watch space movements because when time is running out one way or the other, space movements will show a reversal by breaking back over 1/4, 1/3, or 1/2 of the distance of the last move, which indicates the main trend has changed.

HOW TO USE ANGLES FROM TOPS AND BOTTOMS

The angles to be used from a bottom of a stock up start from the point marked "O" and those starting down from the top of the chart marked "T" are the way they are put on from the top running down. Remember, the first thing to do when you want to put angles on from bottom to top is to draw the angle of 45°, then draw next the angle of 2 x 1 on each side of the 45° angle. In many cases, you will not have to use any other angles for a long time, then put on the other angles when they are necessary. Of course, if your stock is advancing very rapidly, then keep your 1 x 4 angle on and your 8 x 1. The same applies when it is having a sharp decline--keep your angle of 8 x 1 and 4 x 1 drawn down, using the scale of 1 point to each 1/8 of an inch, as shown on your Pattern Chart.

A stock to keep above the 45° angle must make a gain of one point per month, i. e. it must raise its bottoms one point per month. To keep above the angle of 8 x 1 going up, it must raise its bottoms eight points per month, and to keep above the angle of 4 x 1 it must raise its bottoms four points per month. To keep above the angle of 3 x 1, it must raise its bottoms three points per month, and to keep above the angle of 2 x 3 it must raise its bottoms 1½ points per month or make a gain of 18 points per year. On the left hand side of the angle of 45°, beginning with the angle of 6 x 1, the stock only has to make a gain of 2 points per year. If a stock cannot rise above an angle of this kind, it is in a very weak position and of course on the bear side of the square.

The angle to the left of the angle of 3 x 1 indicates a gain of 3 points per year and the angle of 3 x 1 indicates a gain of 4 points per year. The next angle of 2 x 1 indicates a gain of 6 points per year or 1/2 point per month.

Coming down after having broken the angle of 45° and breaking this angle, a stock is in a very weak position, especially if it is a long ways from the base, and indicates much lower prices.

The angle of 3 x 2 on the left rises at the rate of 2 points in 12 months or a gain of 3/4 of a point per month in order to keep above this angle. It is not necessary to draw angles from a long ways back. You can make the calculation and determine where they cross. For example: Suppose in 1900, in the month of January, a stock made bottom at 15, and I want to calculate where the 45° angle will cross 20 years later in January, 1930. The 45° angle rises at the rate of 1 point per month, then 10 years would be 120 months or 120 points added to 15 at the bottom; the 45° angle would cross at 135 in January, 1930. All of the other angles may be calculated in a long way back in the same way.

I have marked on the Pattern Chart the measured degrees of the angles, which you will see are 3¾°, 7½°, 15°, 18¾°, 26¼°, 30°, 33¾°, 37½°, 45°, 52½°, 56¼°, 60°, 63¾°, 71¼°, 75°, 82½°, 86¼°, and 90°. You do not have to bother about measuring these angles. All you have to do to get the angles correct is to count the spaces and draw your lines or angles accordingly.

You will notice on your Pattern Chart how each angle drawn from the top and from the bottom prove themselves by the point at which they cross. For example: The angle of 8 x 1 drawn from "0" and the angle of 8 x 1 drawn from 90 down both cross at 45, 5-5/8 ints over from "0" counting to the right. Then take the angle of x 1 from "0" and 4 x 1 down from 90 and you will notice that they cross at 11¼ on 45, equal distance from the other angle and of course twice the measure.

The reason why these angles prove this way is because the 45° angle or 45 points, degrees, or anything else from "0" to 45 is one-half of 90. Therefore parallel angles beginning at "0" going up and at 90 coming down, must cross on a 45° angle or at the gravity center.

RULES FOR ANGLES FROM BOTTOMS

From any bottom, base or beginning point, two 45° angles can be started, one running up from the vertical angle and one running down from the vertical angle. You can also use a 45° angle or any other angle from any top, running the 45° angle down from the top, which indicates a decline of 1 point per month, week or day, according to your scale of prices; then running the 45° angle up from the top, which would indicate a gain of 1 point or 1 degree per month.

For example: Take the low of U. S. Steel on November 13, 1929, when it sold at 150. Start the 45° angle up and it gains 1 point per month; then start the 45° angle down from 150 and the stock has to decline 1 point per month to rest on the angle of 45°.

November, 1930, was 12 months from November, 1929, and S. Steel made low in November, 1930 at 138, which was on a 45° angle from the bottom at 150.

In December, 1930, U. S. Steel made an extreme low of 134-3/8. This was 2 points under the 45° angle from 150, but rested on the angle of 2 x 1 from the low at 111¼, made in January, 1927. In December, 1930, U. S. Steel closed above the 45° angle from the bottom of 150. As long as it stays above this angle, it is in a stronger position, but to regain the strongest position, it will have to cross the angles of 45° from 150 on the up side and stay above this angle.

Remember that when any stock breaks under the 45° angle on the daily, weekly or monthly puts it in a very weak position and indicates a decline to the next angle. However, when a stock can regain the 45° angle, it is in a stronger position. The same rule applies to a 45° angle up from any top. When a stock crosses the angle on the daily, weekly or monthly and stays above the 45° angle, it is in a very strong position.

After a stock once drops below or gets above any important angle and then reverses its position by getting back above the angle or dropping back below it, it changes the trend again.

The angles on the Monthly and Weekly charts are, of course, of greater importance than those on the Daily charts, because the daily trend can change quite often, while only the major changes are shown according to the angles on the monthly high and low and weekly high and low charts.

Always consider the distance a stock is from its base or beginning point when it breaks any important angle or crosses any important angle. The farther away from the base, the important the change in trend, whether this be crossing an angle from the top or breaking under an angle from the bottom.

Each stock works out its own square according to its extreme high and low points or the square of its tops. For example: U. S. Rubber-- 143 was the total high to measure the width; then move over 143 spaces or 143 months to the angle of 90° down and divide up the square, as I have done on the monthly high and low chart. You can see how it worked out to the 1/4 of its square, 1/2, 3/4, 1/3, 2/3, etc. It will require 143 months to pass out of the square, or 11 years and 11 months. This period of time will end in December, 1931, which will be an important point to watch for a change in trend on U. S. Rubber.

WHY GEOMETRICAL ANGLES WORK ON STOCKS

Why is the 90° angle the strongest angle of all? Because it is horizontal or straight up and straight down.

What is the next strongest angle to the 90° angle? The 180° angle because it is square to the 90° angle, being 90° from the 90° angle.

What is the next strongest angle to the 180° angle? 270 because it is in opposition to 90, or 180° from the 90° angle, which equals 1/2 of the circle, the strongest point.

What is the next strongest angle after 270? 360 because it ends the circle and gets back to the beginning point and is opposite 180° or half-way point, or the angle which equals 1/2 of the circle.

What angles are next strongest to 90, 180, 270 and 360? 120° and 240° because they are 1/3 and 2/3 of the circle. 120 is 90 plus 30, which is 1/3 of 90. 240 is 180 plus 1/3 or 60, which makes those strong angles, especially strong for measurements of time.

What angles are next in strength? 45, because it is 1/2 of 90, and 135 because it is 90 from 45, and 225 because it is 45° from 180, and 315 because it is 45 from 270. The angle of 225° is 180 from 45 and the angle of 315° is 180 from 135.

The angles of 90, 180, 270 and 360 form the first important cross, known as the Cardinal Cross. The angles of 45, 135, 225 and 315 form the next important cross, which is known as the Fixed Cross. These angles are very important for the measurements of time and space and volume.

Why is the angle of 22½° stronger than 11¼°. Because it is twice as much, being the same reason that a 45° angle is stronger than a 22½. Again the angle of 67½ is 1½ times 45, therefore quite strong when anything is moving up toward 90°. 78¾ is stronger than 67½ because it is 7/8 of 90 and therefore one of the strongest points before we reach 90 and important to watch both on time, space and volume. Many stocks have important moves and make tops or bottoms around the 78th to 80th week, month or day.

Why are the angles of 1/8 of a circle most important for time and space measurement? Because we divide $1 into 1/4, 1/2, and 1/8 parts. We use 25¢ or one quarter, 50/ or 1/2 dollar, and long years ago we had 12½¢ pieces. But the most important figures of our basis of money are the four quarters, but we do use the 1/8 part or 12¢ in all calculations. Stock fluctuations are based on 1/8, 1/4, 3/8, 1/2, 5/8, 3/4, 7/8 and the whole figure. Therefore, any space measurement, as well as time, will work out closer to these figures when changed into angles of time than 1/3 or 2/3 points for the simple reason that the fluctuations moving in 1/8 proportion must come out closer to these figures. Figuring $100, or par, as a basis for stock prices and changing these prices to degrees, 12½ would equal 45°, 25 would equal 90°, 37½ would equal 135°, 50 would equal 180°, 62½ would equal 225°, 75 would equal 270°, 82½ would equal 315°, and 100 would equal 360°.

For example: When a stock sells at 50 on the 180th day, week or month, it is on the degree of its time angle. On February 1, 1915, U. S. Steel made a low at 38, which is closest to a price of 37½, which is 3/8 of 100 and equals a 135° angle. Steel was 14 years old or 168 months old on February 25, 1915 and hit the angle of 135°

which showed that Steel was behind time, but that it was in a strong position holding at 38 above the angle of 135°, or the price of 37½. Then when Steel crossed 200, it equalled 2 circles of 360°. When it advanced to 261⅝, it was closest to 62½ in the third 100 or nearest the 225° angle. It was the strongest angle after it crossed the half-way point or 180° angle. Steel's half-way point on the third hundred was 250; 262½ would be the next point, or 5/8 point, which equals 225°.

Under the instructions for the Master Timing Angles, you will find how far each timing angle had moved from the time Steel was incorporated up to the time it made extreme top. Study these timing angles and you will see what happens when each of the timing angles reach 24, 36, 48, 60, 72, 84, 90, 120, 135, 157½, 180, 210, 225, 240, 270, 300, 315, 330, 345, and 360 months, the equivalent of 360°. Under the Master Timing Angles we also show you what happens when timing angles #5, 6, 7, 8, and 9 cross the other timing angles, or the place where they were at the time Steel was incorporated. Of course these same rules can be applied to any other stock. You can see what happens when each of these Master Timing Angles returns to the same place it was at the time Steel was incorporated, or to the same place when any extreme high or low price is reached. You will learn when these Master Timing Angles return to the same place or to the same angle or degree from which they started. Therefore you will know the exact measurements of cycles according to moving energy. The instructions on the Master Timing Angles give you the cause of all market movements and they can be worked out ahead as far as the year 2000. The figures which we will use are figures made by the United States Government astronomers and are therefore absolutely accurate. A careful study of all these figures and a comparison of the movements of the various stocks will convince you of their value.

HOW TO USE GEOMETRICAL ANGLES

My Method of operating in the Stock Market is all based on mathematical points or geometrical angles. The Resistance Levels are all geometrical angles because they are 1/8, 1/4, 1/2, 3/4, 1/3, 2/3, etc., which are proportional parts of a circle whether large or small and, therefore, represent geometrical angles.

There are three important factors to consider, price, time and space movements. For example, when the price reaches 45, it meets resistance because it is equal to a 45° angle. Then when the price breaks a 45° angle, regardless of whether the price is at 45, 67, 90, 135, 180 or anywhere else, it weakens the position and equals a resistance angle, but is more important when a long ways from the base. The distance the stock breaks the angle of 45° or any other angle from the base is the most important. For example, many times a stock will rest on the angle of 45° in its early stages when advancing, then later in reaction rests on it again, then have a prolonged advance, react and rest on the 45° angle again, and then hit a higher level, break the 45° angle the fourth time, which places it in an extremely weak position because it is so far away from the base and so much time has elapsed since the stock made low level. Reverse this rule in a bear market or a decline and don't forget to consider that the Monthly and Weekly high and low charts are the most important when angles are broken. Daily charts can break angles and recover them and it is impossible for a daily high and low chart to maintain an angle of 45° for a very long period of time except when the final grand rush comes at the end of big bull campaigns.

Suppose at the time a stock breaks a 45° angle that it is at 135, and on the 135th month. This would be at a strong Resistance Level, breaking a strong angle, and striking and breaking a strong angle according to time. This would be time and space balancing at Resistance Levels, or geometrical angles, and would indicate a big decline to follow. Reverse the same rule at the end of a bear campaign.

After considering the three important factors, Resistance Levels, time and geometrical angles, the fourth and next very important factor is the volume of sales at tops or bottoms. Sales increase near the top and decrease near the bottom, that is, when a bear campaign has run for a long time and liquidation has about run its course, the volume of sales decrease, which is an indication that the market is getting ready to make a change in trend.

VANADIUM STEEL, WEEKLY HIGH & LOW CHART, VOLUME OF SALES.

This chart begins September 29, 1928. For each space 1/8 wide, I have used to represent 25,000 shares. For example, during the week ending September 29, 1928, sales were 26,600 shares and the high was 85 and the low 76 which is represented by 1/8. The same with the following week, when sales were 25,000 shares or less and the stock remained in a narrow trading range but gradually worked up until the week ending October 27th, when the volume of sales was 111,400 shares and the stock advanced to 88½. I made the space 4 wide to represent 100,000 shares. Then note November 10th, or the week ending November 10th, when the stock advanced from 84½ to 108, sales were 238,900 shares. The following week, sales were, 116,400 shares and the price only went 3 points higher. Then the stock broke the angle of 45° and declined to 85. During the week ending December 8th, and the following week, the price was around this same level, holding above the angle of 4 x 1 from the bottom, and failing to get back to the low reached during the week ending December 10th. The volume of sales on this decline was small. For the week ending December 22nd, sales were only 25,000 shares. Then the stock started up again.

During the week ending January 19, 1929, sales were 138,800. The following week sales were 61,200 and the next week with the stock getting only ½ point lower, sales were only 25,000 shares. Then followed a quick rally ending in the week of February 9th, with sales of 175,000 shares. This was top. A quick reation followed with sales of 74,200 shares. In the following week, the bottom was around the same level with sales of 153,000 shares. During the week ending March 2nd, sales were 51,500 shares. Then followed two weeks of small volume, 33,500 shares and 32,200 shares. Here the stock again broke under the angle of 22½, or 2 x 1 from the level of September 29, 1928 and a decline followed. Bottom was reached at 68 on the week ending June 1st, when sales were only 33,700 shares. The following week sales were only 27,000 shares which indicated that liquidation was not heavy and had run its course. The stock rallied to 97 during the week ending July 20th. The volume of sales was only 48,700 shares, not enough volume to indicate that the buying was strong enough to force the stock higher at that time. A decline followed and the volume of sales was small. Bottom was reached during the week ending August 10th at 77½. During those weeks the sales run 25,000 or less, getting down to 8,800 during the week ending August 31st which indicated that there was not much stock for sale at this price and that some one was just taking what was offered.

During the week ending September 14th, the stock was rushed up to 100 on sales of 138,400. Note that it failed to cross the top of April 6th, and that both of these tops were under the heavy volume of February 16th and 23rd, which indicated the big distribution that took place between 104 and 115 was by people who did not intend to buy the stock back for a long time and that when the stock approached the level of 100, they sold heavily again.

During the week ending September 28th, a decline followed on small volume, but the angle of 45° was broken and the stock continued to work lower. The volume increased during the week ending October 26th to 56,600 shares. The following week it was 50,600 shares, indicating heavy liquidation at this time. Then during the week ending November 9th and 16th, sales dropped to 17,200 shares and 29,000 shares. Final bottom was reached on November 13th at 37½. Then a rally followed up to the week ending December 14th, but the volume of sales was small only getting up to 31,000 shares and on the top week 21,000 shares. A reaction followed but the volume of sales was still smaller, 12,300, 11,300, and 13,800 shares. The bottom was reached during the week ending December 21st, when sales were 19,000 shares, then two narrow weeks on the side with the total volume not exceeding 25,000 shares. This indicated that the stock was thoroughly liquidated and was getting ready to go higher, but the week ending February 1, 1930, when the stock crossed the high of December 14th, volume of sales increased to 92,000 shares. Then during the week of February 8, there was a small reaction, but the volume of sales was only 23,000 shares. The advanced was resumed the following week and sales reached 62,400 shares. The next week the sales were 48,300 shares. Then during the week ending March 1, there was a small reaction but the volume of sales were only 36,500 shares which indicated that the buying was better than the selling, and that there was no heavy selling pressure yet. The advance was resumed and the volume of sales increased every week until the week ending March 29, when the stock sold at 124½ with a volume of sales of 206,000 shares. This was the largest volume of sales of any time since November 1928, a reaction of 20 points followed, but during the week ending April 5th, sales were only 83,600 shares. In the following week the stock made a higher bottom showing that the market had not yet reached top.

During the week ending April 19th, sales were 184,600 shares and during the week ending April 26th, sales were 258,100 shares. With the stock up 105 points from the extreme low, and the volume of sales almost equalling the total amount of stock outstanding, was a plain indication that top was being reached for a big reaction. During the week ending May 3rd a big decline followed sales reached 304,000 shares, an angle of 45° from the low at 103½ was first broken, then the angle of 45° from 37½ was broken and the stock declined to 87 during the week ending May 10th on sales of 310,400 shares, breaking all records up to that time. It got down near the angle of 22½°, or the angle of 2 x 1 from the low of 37½. It was a big reaction for two weeks period of time and came down 57 points. Figuring your low of 37½ to the high of 143¼, gives a half-way point of 90 3/8. The stock declined 3 3/8 points beyond this. This was due to the large volume of sales and the momentum. However, often a stock will go 3 3/4 points beyond the half-way point and then recover, especially if it has had a big decline. The greater the decline in number of points, the more allowance can be made for fluctuations around the main center or half-way point and, of course, Vanadium with a very small volume of floating supply of stock makes faster moves and wider range than a stock of large volume.

During the week ending May 10th, the volume of sales of 242,400 shares and the price crossed the top of the following week and advanced to 118½. The following week it advanced to 120¾ on sales of 248,600 shares, showing that the volume of trading was increasing on the way up but the price was not increasing in proportion.

During the week ending May 31st, the stock reached 124 on volume of sales of 135,700 shares, an indication that the selling was better than the buying and that when the price level approached where distribution started, it showed that there was again the very best of selling.

During the week ending June 7th, the price advanced to 125. Figuring the top of 143¾ to the low of 87, the 2/3 points was at 126¾. Then figuring the total value of the stock 143¼, we find the 7/8 point at 125 3/8. This made 125 a very strong Resistance Level because it was at the 7/8 point, of total value, and close to the 2/3 point on the fluctuating moves. Another reason why 125 was a strong Resistance Level is because 25 is 1/4 of 100.

During the week ending June 7th, Vanadium broke the angle of 45° from the low of 37 on heavy volume, the total sales for the week being 237,100. The price got down to 100 and rested on the angle of $22\frac{1}{2}°$, or the angle of 2 x 1 from $37\frac{1}{2}$. On June 9th, Vanadium broke 100 and, of course, was under the angle of 2 x 1 and declined to $89\frac{1}{2}$, this time getting support around the gravity center, or half-way point, from $37\frac{1}{2}$ to $143\frac{1}{2}$. However, Vanadium is in a weak position on angles according to the volume chart, and in a weak position on angles according to the weekly chart, without volume, and the Monthly high and low chart and nothing but a rally is indicated at this time. However, if it can hold for a while and not break the low of 37 on May 10th, it will indicate a better rally, probably 1/3 to 1/2 of the recent decline.

From the low on November 13, to the high in April, the total volume of sales was 1,672,600 shares figuring 25,000 to each 1/8 space to move over each week would bring this over to the 67th space, which I have marked, and you will see from the volume chart that this runs over which is due to the fact that some weeks volume did not equal 25,000 shares. We have to register the top and bottom and this throws us out a little on balance. In the weeks of May 3rd and 10th, the total volume was 614,000 shares, bringing the grand total up to that time to 2,282,000 which brings it to space 91, on the week ending May 10th and puts our volume chart 6 spaces too far over. Note that the volume of those two weeks was about 1/3 of the total volume from $37\frac{1}{2}$ to 143 3/4 and, of course, wiped out half of the advance. Therefore, it is only natural that a rally should follow because the decline was too fast according to time. Bringing the total number of sales up to the week ending June 7, we have 3,170,800 shares. This would bring us to space 126, marked in red ink, and the way we have the volume chart, it is 8 spaces too far over. Therefore, the volume for the week ending June 7th, with the space movement rested exactly on the angle of 2 x 1 from $37\frac{1}{2}$, and 101 to $100\frac{3}{8}$ would strike up against this angle on the week beginning June 9th. The price on June 9th was $101\frac{3}{8}$, and the stock declined to $89\frac{1}{2}$. After a stock gets away from a narrow series of fluctuations with small volume and keep your volume chart exact, so as your angles will work out better.

MONTHLY VOLUME CHARTS ON DOW-JONES THIRTY INDUSTRIALS FROM JUNE 1921 to MAY 1930

A study of this volume chart will prove very interesting and valuable. You can see that in June, July and August, 1921, the volume of sales was down to around, 10,000,000 to 15,000,000 shares per month. In March 1928, sales reached 80,000,000 per month for the first time in history. From this time on the volume of sales was very large, with this group of stocks working higher right along from the reaction in June 1928 when the price was 194 to the top in September 1029 when the price reached 381, there was never more than one month's reaction and at no time did the aver-

again break 10 points under a previous month's bottom. The volume of sales increased enormously in October, 1928, and continued large in November, December, and in fact, right on up until August, 1929, when sales were again over 100,000,000 shares, and the month of September sales were over 100,000,000 shares; see how the picture looks with this enormous volume at the top and then in October, the first time since May, 1929, the price broke under the level of the previous month, showing that the trend had turned down. All records for volume of sales was broken in the month of October, when sales reached 141,000,000. In the final reaction in November, or the last wave of liquidation, sales dropped down to around 80,000,000. Then the price worked up every month, making higher bottoms and higher tops with a fairly large volume, until March, 1930, when the volume of sales reached 90,000,000. In April, the total volume of sales reached 111,000,000 shares, a very small gain in price. In the early part of May the price broke under the bottom of the month of April, which was the first time since the low was reached in November, and a sharp decline followed. The volume of sales for the month of May was heavy, reaching 80,000,000; then continued in June on fairly heavy volume, with the price getting down to 250 on June 9th. This movement on volume from November, 1929 to April, 1930, shows a rally in a bear market.

Note the bottom from January, 1929 to May, 1929, and that the rally in April just brought prices up under this heavy volume of sales where distribution took place in 1929. Note that the scale on this chart is 2 points to each 1/8 of an inch instead of 1, for in considering the angles from the low in August, 1921 and the low in November, 1923, the angles are doubled in value, that is, the angle of 2 x 1 equals the angle of 45° and the angle of 4 x 1 equals the angle of 2 x 1 or 22½°. For example, the angle of 2 x 1 from the low in June, 1928 equals the angle of 45°. Note that the price rested on this angle in May, 1929, and that it was broken for the first time in October, 1929 and the big decline followed. Note that the angle of 4 x 1 from August, 1921, which is the equal of the angle of 22½°, or 2 x 1, fairly in April, 1930, come right up under this angle. Then consider the next angle of 4 x 1 from November, 1923, which is also equal to the angle of 22½°, notice prices in March and April got slightly above this angle, but that when the price opened in May, 1930, it dropped under this angle and then broke the angle of 45° from November, 1929 and the angle of 45° is really the angle of 2 x 1, or 22½°, counting the basis of the chart being at the rate of 2 spaces for one. Then the angle of 2 x 1, from November 1929 is equal to the angle of 45°. This angle crosses at 248 in June 1930, the same place where the angle of 2 x 1, from the corner of the top of October, 1919, angle of 2 x 1, or 45 as it is drawn across there, crosses, making 248 a very important point. Also note that the low in January, 1930, was 246. If this angle is broken and this low of 246, of January, is broken, it will indicate very much lower prices for these averages.

FAST ADVANCES AND FAST DECLINES

Why do stocks that have fast advances, reverse quickly and have sharp, quick declines before breaking the angle of 67½°, or the 45° angle on the monthly and weekly charts?

It is because the large volume of sales moves the prices over until the 45° angle is really broken at a very high level, which can be seen by making the combination time, space and volume chart. The volume chart shows that the angle is broken while the time chart, which only shows one space for each month or week, does not show the angle broken.

For example, make up a volume chart on U. S. Steel weekly from May 31, 1929 to date, and you will see that it broke so sharply after the high in September, 1929, because the volume broke the angle before the angles were broken by the weekly or monthly chart.

We are sending you Vanadium weekly from 1929 to date with volume. This will show you how the stock works when volume of sales is charted with time and space.

Why do stocks take such a long time to recover after a long decline and remain so long at low levels?

Because the volume gets so small near the bottom that it requires a long time to overcome the square of distance. When a stock declines 100 points or more in two or three months, for example, we will say exactly 100 points, then to overcome the square of distance at a low level, it requires 100 months. A stock has to square itself on the weekly, monthly and daily high and low chart. The lower the price crosses the 45° angle, the stronger the position of the stock and the higher the stock is and the greatest distance from the base, or beginning point when the 45° angle is broken or, in fact, any other angle, the weaker the stock is.

Why do stocks often cross the 45° angle on the daily, weekly or monthly high and low chart, then have an advance for a short period of time, decline and rest on the 45° angle?

It is because when they cross the 45° angle the first time, they have crossed it before they have run out or overcome the square of distance. Therefore, on the secondary reaction, when they rest on the 45° angle, it is at a time when they have reached the square of distance, and after that time a greater advance follows. Reverse this rule at the top of a bull market. This accounts for the stocks having a sharp, quick decline from the top and then advancing and making a slightly higher top or a series of slightly lower tops, working over until it overcomes the square of distance at a comparatively high level and breaks the 45° angle, then a fast decline follows.

What rule should be followed when stocks make higher bottoms and lower tops?

As stocks advance and make higher bottoms on the monthly, weekly or daily chart, you should always draw angles from higher bottoms. Then when you reach the last section of a bull market, and those important angles are broken from the last bottom, you know that the trend has turned down, Apply this same rule as a market declines. Draw your angles from each lower top and watch your angles until the stocks again cross the 45° angle from a second, third, or fourth lower top. The second lower top, or second higher bottom is always very important to draw angles from, and to measure time from, as well.

When a stock is in a very weak, or a very strong position, it will always show it by its position on angles, and a volume chart, made up according to the proper spacing with volume, that is, considering the total number of shares, will show when the stock is in a strong or weak position and show whether buying or selling predominates, enabling you to determine whether supply is increasing, or whether demand is decreasing.

WHAT RULE TO USE WHEN IN DOUBT

When you are in doubt about the position of a stock and do not know what its trend is, you should, of course, not trade in it. Wait until it shows by breaking resistance level, or crossing a resistance level, or until it crosses an important angle, or breaks an important angle before deciding which way it is going to move, especially after it has been in a long deadlock, or in a sideways movement, as referred to in "Wall Street Stock Selector." As a general rule, when a change in trend takes place of importance, the volume of sales will show it. The volume of sales usually increases when a stock starts to advance from low levels, or from dullness, and the same after a long period of dullness at a high level, when activity starts on the down side, the volume of sales increases. When a stock starts up and is in a strong position, it will show it on angles by keeping above strong angles from the bottom. The same when it starts to decline. If it is in a very weak position and going very fast, it will show it by the position of angles, that is, dropping below and keeping below strong angles, With the daily, weekly and monthly high and low chart, the important angles cannot be crossed at extreme low levels, until proper time has elapsed, neither can important angles be broken at high levels until sufficient time has elapsed. Therefore, the angles are very important because when broken they usually mean that the time has run out, whether you know it or not, and a change in trend will take place.

MASTER "12" CHART

The MASTER CHART is the Square of "12" or 12 x 12, making the first square end at 144. The Second Square of "12" ends at 288, the Third Square of "12" at 432, and the Fourth Square at 576, which will cover most anything that you want, but you can make up as many more squares as you want.

This chart may be used and applies to anything-- TIME,

During the week ending June 7th, Vanadium broke the angle of 45° from the low of 37 on heavy volume, the total sales for the week being 237,100. The price got down to 100 and rested on the angle of $22\frac{1}{2}°$, or the angle of 2 x 1 from $37\frac{1}{2}$. On June 9th, Vanadium broke 100 and, of course, was under the angle of 2 x 1 and declined to $89\frac{1}{2}$, this time getting support around the gravity center, or half-way point, from $37\frac{1}{2}$ to $143\frac{1}{2}$. However, Vanadium is in a weak position on angles according to the volume chart, and in a weak position on angles according to the weekly chart, without volume, and the Monthly high and low chart and nothing but a rally is indicated at this time. However, if it can hold for a while and not break the low of 37 on May 10th, it will indicate a better rally, probably 1/3 to 1/2 of the recent decline.

From the low on November 13, to the high in April, the total volume of sales was 1,672,600 shares figuring 25,000 to each 1/8 space to move over each week would bring this over to the 67th space, which I have marked, and you will see from the volume chart that this runs over which is due to the fact that some weeks volume did not equal 25,000 shares. We have to register the top and bottom and this throws us out a little on balance. In the weeks of May 3rd and 10th, the total volume was 614,000 shares, bringing the grand total up to that time to 2,282,000 which brings it to space 91, on the week ending May 10th and puts our volume chart 6 spaces too far over. Note that the volume of these two weeks was about 1/3 of the total volume from $37\frac{1}{2}$ to 143 3/4 and, of course, wiped out half of the advance. Therefore, it is only natural that a rally should follow because the decline was too fast according to time. Bringing the total number of sales up to the week ending June 7, we have 3,170,800 shares. This would bring us to space 126, marked in red ink, and the way we have the volume chart, it is 8 spaces too far over. Therefore, the volume for the week ending June 7th, with the space movement rested exactly on the angle of 2 x 1 from $37\frac{1}{2}$, and 101 to $100\frac{3}{4}$ would strike up against this angle on the week beginning June 9th. The price on June 9th was $101\frac{1}{2}$, and the stock declined to $89\frac{1}{2}$. After a stock gets away from a narrow series of fluctuations with small volume and keep your volume chart exact, so as your angles will work out better.

MONTHLY VOLUME CHARTS ON DOW-JONES THIRTY INDUSTRIALS FROM JUNE 1921 to MAY 1930

A study of this volume chart will prove very interesting and valuable. You can see that in June, July and August, 1921, the volume of sales was down to around, 10,000,000 to 15,000,000 shares per month. In March 1928, sales reached 80,000,000 per month for the first time in history. From this time on the volume of sales was very large, with this group of stocks working higher right along from the reaction in June 1928 when the price was 194 to the top in September 1929 when the price reached 381, there was never more than one month's reaction and at no time did the aver-

again break 10 points under a previous month's bottom. The volume of sales increased enormously in October, 1928, and continued large in November, December, and in fact, right on up until August, 1929, when sales were again over 100,000,000 shares, and the month of September sales were over 100,000,000 shares; see how the picture looks with this enormous volume at the top and then in October, the first time since May, 1929, the price broke under the level of the previous month, showing that the trend had turned down. All records for volume of sales was broken in the month of October, when sales reached 141,000,000. In the final reaction in November, or the last wave of liquidation, sales dropped down to around 80,000,000. Then the price worked up every month, making higher bottoms and higher tops with a fairly large volume, until March, 1930, when the volume of sales reached 90,000,000. In April, the total volume of sales reached 111,000,000 shares, a very small gain in price. In the early part of May the price broke under the bottom of the month of April, which was the first time since the low was reached in November, and a sharp decline followed. The volume of sales for the month of May was heavy, reaching 80,000,000; then continued in June on fairly heavy volume, with the price getting down to 250 on June 9th. This movement on volume from November, 1929 to April, 1930, shows a rally in a bear market.

Note the bottom from January, 1929 to May, 1929, and that the rally in April just brought prices up under this heavy volume of sales where distribution took place in 1929. Note that the scale on this chart is 2 points to each 1/8 of an inch instead of 1, for in considering the angles from the low in August, 1921 and the low in November, 1923, the angles are doubled in value, that is, the angle of 2 x 1 equals the angle of 45° and the angle of 4 x 1 equals the angle of 2 x 1 or 22½°. For example, the angle of 2 x 1 from the low in June, 1928 equals the angle of 45°. Note that the price rested on this angle in May, 1929, and that it was broken for the first time in October, 1929 and the big decline followed. Note that the angle of 4 x 1 from August, 1921, which is the equal of the angle of 22½°, or 2 x 1, fairly in April, 1930, come right up under this angle. Then consider the next angle of 4 x 1 from November, 1923, which is also equal to the angle of 22½°, notice prices in March and April got slightly above this angle, but that when the price opened in May, 1930, it dropped under this angle and then broke the angle of 45° from November, 1929 and the angle of 45° is really the angle of 2 x 1, or 22½°, counting the basis of the chart being at the rate of 2 spaces for one. Then the angle of 2 x 1, from November 1929 is equal to the angle of 45°. This angle crosses at 248 in June 1930, the same place where the angle of 2 x 1, from the corner of the top of October, 1919, angle of 2 x 1, or 45 as it is drawn across there, crosses, making 248 a very important point. Also note that the low in January, 1930, was 246. If this angle is broken and this low of 246, of January, is broken, it will indicate very much lower prices for these averages.

FAST ADVANCES AND FAST DECLINES

Why do stocks that have fast advances, reverse quickly and have sharp, quick declines before breaking the angle of 67½°, or the 45° angle on the monthly and weekly charts?

It is because the large volume of sales moves the prices over until the 45° angle is really broken at a very high level, which can be seen by making the combination time, space and volume chart. The volume chart shows that the angle is broken while the time chart, which only shows one space for each month or week, does not show the angle broken.

For example, make up a volume chart on U. S. Steel weekly from May 31, 1929 to date, and you will see that it broke so sharply after the high in September, 1929, because the volume broke the angle before the angles were broken by the weekly or monthly chart.

We are sending you Vanadium weekly from 1929 to date with volume. This will show you how the stock works when volume of sales is charted with time and space.

Why do stocks take such a long time to recover after a long decline and remain so long at low levels?

Because the volume gets so small near the bottom that it requires a long time to overcome the square of distance. When a stock declines 100 points or more in two or three months, for example, we will say exactly 100 points, then to overcome the square of distance at a low level, it requires 100 months. A stock has to square itself on the weekly, monthly and daily high and low chart. The lower the price crosses the 45° angle, the stronger the position of the stock and the higher the stock is and the greatest distance from the base, or beginning point when the 45° angle is broken or, in fact, any other angle, the weaker the stock is.

Why do stocks often cross the 45° angle on the daily, weekly or monthly high and low chart, then have an advance for a short period of time, decline and rest on the 45° angle?

It is because when they cross the 45° angle the first time, they have crossed it before they have run out or overcome the square of distance. Therefore, on the secondary reaction, when they rest on the 45° angle, it is at a time when they have reached the square of distance, and after that time a greater advance follows. Reverse this rule at the top of a bull market. This accounts for the stocks having a sharp, quick decline from the top and then advancing and making a slightly higher top or a series of slightly lower tops, working over until it overcomes the square of distance at a comparatively high level and breaks the 45° angle, then a fast decline follows.

What rule should be followed when stocks make higher bottoms and lower tops?

As stocks advance and make higher bottoms on the monthly, weekly or daily chart, you should always draw angles from higher bottoms. Then when you reach the last section of a bull market, and those important angles are broken from the last bottom, you know that the trend has turned down, Apply this same rule as a market declines. Draw your angles from each lower top and watch your angles until the stocks again cross the 45° angle from a second, third, or fourth lower top. The second lower top, or second higher bottom is always very important to draw angles from, and to measure time from, as well.

When a stock is in a very weak, or a very strong position, it will always show it by its position on angles, and a volume chart, made up according to the proper spacing with volume, that is, considering the total number of shares, will show when the stock is in a strong or weak position and show whether buying or selling predominates, enabling you to determine whether supply is increasing, or whether demand is decreasing.

WHAT RULE TO USE WHEN IN DOUBT

When you are in doubt about the position of a stock and do not know what its trend is, you should, of course, not trade in it. Wait until it shows by breaking resistance level, or crossing a resistance level, or until it crosses an important angle, or breaks an important angle before deciding which way it is going to move, especially after it has been in a long deadlock, or in a sideways movement, as referred to in "Wall Street Stock Selector." As a general rule, when a change in trend takes place of importance, the volume of sales will show it. The volume of sales usually increases when a stock starts to advance from low levels, or from dullness, and the same after a long period of dullness at a high level, when activity starts on the down side, the volume of sales increases. When a stock starts up and is in a strong position, it will show it on angles by keeping above strong angles from the bottom. The same when it starts to decline. If it is in a very weak position and going very fast, it will show it by the position of angles, that is, dropping below and keeping below strong angles, With the daily, weekly and monthly high and low chart, the important angles cannot be crossed at extreme low levels, until proper time has elapsed, neither can important angles be broken at high levels until sufficient time has elapsed. Therefore, the angles are very important because when broken they usually mean that the time has run out, whether you know it or not, and a change in trend will take place.

MASTER "12" CHART

The MASTER CHART is the Square of "12" or 12 x 12, making the first square end at 144. The Second Square of "12" ends at 288, the Third Square of "12" at 432, and the Fourth Square at 576, which will cover most anything that you want, but you can make up as many more squares as you want.

This chart may be used and applies to anything-- TIME,

SPACE OR VOLUME, the number of points up or down; days, weeks, months and years.

On Square No. 1, which runs from 1 to 144, I have drawn the finer angles to show the grand-center or strongest Resistance Point in each minor square. The minor centers, which are the strongest for minor tops and bottoms are 14, 17, 20, 23, 50, 53, 56, 59, 86, 89, 92, 95, 122, 125, 128, 131.

The major center is where the strongest resistance is met. These numbers are 66, 67, 78, and 79. Stocks going up or coming down to these prices will meet with stubborn resistance. The next strong angle is the 45°, and the numbers of greatest resistance are 14, 27, 40, 63, 66, 79, 92, 105, 118, 131, and 144. The other diagonal 45° angle from 12 is equally strong. The numbers are 12, 23, 34, 45, 67, 78, 89, 100, 111, 122 and 133.

The numbers which are cut by the 45° angles thru the center of each of the 1/4 squares are next in strength. These numbers are 7, 20, 43, 46, 59, 72, 61, 56, 30, 28, 17 and 6, and on the other side of the Square, after you pass the half-way point, these numbers are 75, 86, 99, 112, 125, 138, 139, 128, 117, 106, 95 and 84.

The numbers at the tops and bottoms of the squares are important prices for important tops and bottoms to be made because they are opposition numbers and are equal to the half-way point. These numbers for Square No. 1 are 1, 13, 25, 37, 49, 61, 73, 85, 97, 109, 121, 135. The top numbers are 12, 24, 36, 48, 60, 72, 84, 96, 108, 120, 132 and 144.

The opposition angle, which runs thru the center of the Square, from east to west, equally dividing it, is one of the very strong angles because it equals one-half. Any stock moving up or down and reaching these prices will meet with resistance and make tops or bottoms. These numbers are 6, 7, 18, 19, 30, 31, 42, 43, 54, 55, 66, 67, 78, 79, 90, 91, 102, 103, 114, 115, 126, 127, 138, 139.

Remember, when anything has moved three sections over from the beginning, it reaches the square of its own place, which is the first strong resistance. When it has moved six sections over, it reaches the opposition, or what equals the half-way point of its own place and meets still stronger resistance. Moving over nine places or sections from its own place, it reaches the 3/4 point, another square. The 8th and 9th sections are the strongest and hardest points to pass because this is the "death" zone. The next and still stronger is the 12th section or column which ends at 144. Anything getting into this section meets the strongest resistance but once it moves out of this Square and gets as much as 3 points into Square #2, that is, making 147, will indicate much higher, But after reaching this, it should not drop back 3 points or to 141 in Square #1.

When a stock gets into the Second Square of "12", it has faster moves, and when the time or number of months from any bottom or top moves into the Second Square, it is an indication of faster moves, both up and down.

Apply the same rule to the 3rd, 4th, 5th and 6th Squares, In the 3rd and 4th Squares of the Master "12", you will find that most of the big bull and bear campaigns culminate, when measured by months, which determines the division, according to time. All of the other rules given you to apply to Space movements, angles and time, can be used with the Master "12" tables.

SQUARE OF NINE

You have already had the MASTER SQUARE OF TWELVE explained, which represents days, weeks, months and years, and the measurements of TIME in the Square of Twelve or the Square of the Circle.

The SQUARE OF NINE is very important because nine digits are used in measuring everything, and we cannot go beyond 9 without starting to repeat and using the 0. If we divide 360° by 9, we get 40, which measures 40°, 40 months, 40 days, or 40 weeks, and shows why bottoms and tops often come out on these angles measured by one-ninth of the total circle.

If we divide our 20-year period, or 240 months, by 9, we get 26-2/3 months, making an important angle of 26-2/3°, months, days or weeks. Nine times 9 equals 81, which completes the First Square of Nine. Note the angles and how they run from the main center. The Second Square of Nine is completed at 162. Note how this is in opposition to the main center. The Third Square of Nine is completed at 243, which would equal 243 months or 3 months over our 20-year period and accounts for the time which often elapses before the change in the Cycle, sometimes running over 3 months or more. The Fourth Square of Nine ends at 324. Note the angles of 45° cross at 325, indicating a change in cycles here. To complete the 360° requires Four Squares of Nine and 36 over. Note that 361 equals a Square of 19 times 19, thus proving the great value of the Square of Nine in working out the important angles and proving up discrepancies.

Beginning with "1" at the center, note how 7, 21, 43, 75, 111, 157, 211, 273 and 343 all fall on a 45° angle. Going the other way, note that 3, 13, 31, 57, 91, 133, 183, 241 and 307 fall on an angle of 45°. Remember there are always four ways you can travel from a center following an angle of 45°, or an angle of 180° or an angle of 90°, which all equal about the same when measured on a flat surface. Note that 8, 23, 46, 77, 116 163, 218, 281 and 353 are all on an angle from the main center also note that 4, 15, 34, 61, 96, 139, 190, 249 and 316 are on an angle from the main center, all of these being great resistance points and measuring out important time factors and angles.

Study the SQUARE OF NINE very carefully in connection with the MASTER TWELVE and 360° CIRCLE CHART.

SIX SQUARES OF NINE

We are sending you six Permanent Charts, each containing 81 numbers. The First Square of Nine runs from 1 to 81. Everything must have a bottom, top, and four sides to be a square or cube. The First Square running up to 81 is the bottom, base, floor or beginning point. Squares #2, 3, 4 and 5 are the four sides, which are equal and contain 81 numbers. The Sixth Square of Nine is the top and means that it is times times as referred to in the Bible, or a thing reproducting itself by being multiplied by itself. Nine times nine equals 81 and six times 81 equals 486. We can also use 9 times 81, which would equal 729.

The number 5 is the most important number of the digits because it is the balance or main center. There are four numbers on each side of it. Note how it is shown as the balancing or center number in the Square of Nine.

We square the Circle by beginning at 1 in the center and going around until we reach 360. Note that the Square of Nine comes out at 361. The reason for this is it is 19 times, and the 1 to begin with and one over 360 represent the beginning and ending points. 361 is a transition point and begins at the next circle. Should we leave the first space blank or make it "O", then we would come out at 360. Everything in mathematics must prove. You can begin at the center and work out, or begin at the outer rim and work in to the center. Begin at the left and work right to the center or to the outer rim or square.

Note the Square of Nine or the Square of the Circle where we begin with 1 and run up the side of the column to 19, then continue to go across until we have made 19 columns, again the square of 19 by 19. Note how this proves up the circle. One-half of the circle is 180°. Note that in the grand-center, where all angles from the four corners and from the East, West, North and South reach gravity center, number 191 appears, showing that this point we are crossing the Equator or Gravity center and are starting on the other half of the circle.

We have astronomical and astrological proof of the whys and wherefores and the cause of the workings of geometrical angles. When you have made progress, proved yourself worthy, I will give you the Master Number and also the Master Work.

Study the human body in every way and you will find that it is the work of a Master Mind, and when once you know yourself and know your body, you will know the Law and will understand all there is to know. Remember there is a source of all supply, and that you have within you the power to know all there is to know, but you must work hard, seek and you shall find.

CHAPTER 2

THE HUMAN BODY AND TIME CYCLES

THE HUMAN BODY

There are seven openings in the head-- two eyes, two ears and two nostrils, equally divided, three on each side. From this we get our Law of Three and know the reason why the change comes after two and in the third period. The seventh opening in the head is the mouth and everything goes down. Study your seven-year periods and see how your markets go down and make tops and bottoms.

Woman is more perfect than man because she can create. Her body contains 12 openings. Man's body only contains 11. The 12 represents the 12 signs of the Zodiac. The fact that man's body only contains 11 openings proves why a man betrayed Christ and not a woman. Note the angle of $11\frac{1}{4}^{\circ}$. Note the number 11 on all of your different charts. Study the position of 7 times 7 or 49 on all of your permanent charts. Then you will understand why the children of Israel marched 7 times around the walls of Jericho, blew the ram's horn 7 times and the walls fell down on the 7th day. This Law is also backed with astrological proof, but anything that can be proved in any way or by any science is not correct unless it can be proved by numbers and by geometry.

The Time Cycles and every measurement of angles are represented by the human body. You have 5 fingers on each hand/ They are above the waistline or solar plexus and represent the 10-year cycle or the two 5-year cycles, which are 1/4 and 1/2 of the 20 year cycles. You have 10 toes, but note that there are 5 on one side and 5 on the other. This indicates that one 10-year cycle which is below the base line, must run opposite to the 10 above the base line, but that the 10 and 20-year tops and bottoms will come out according to the proper measurements from the base or beginning point. Study the different divisions of your limbs. Note the 3 divisions of your fingers, and that the third joint or ends of your fingers are shorter than the other two, and that the thumb really contains only two spaces or joints, where your fingers contain 3, Learn the secret of this and you will learn why the thumb is so important. Study all of these Master charts, apply them to Space, Time and you will find the cause of tops and bottoms and will know how to determine Resistance Levels. Go back over any of the old charts you have and study the places where they have had the greatest resistance. Note the price, then determine the time by weeks, months or days, and you will be able to learn how to understand future movements. Look up the position of your Master Twelve Chart and your Square of Nine, then consider your geometrical angles from West to East, according to time, then consider your angles from the different bases or beginning points and you will be able to determine the position of a stock.

The SQUARE OF NINE, the MASTER TWELVE SQUARE, and the GEOMETRICAL ANGLES are all mathematical points and do not contradict each other but harmonize and prove up the different mathematical points.

January 17, 1931.

W D Gann

CHAPTER 3

SOY BEANS

PRICE RESISTANCE LEVELS

ACTIVE ANGLES

DEGREES OF ZODIAC

SOY BEANS

PRICE RESISTANCE LEVELS

The one-half point of the highest selling price and one-half between the high and low are very great because these equal the 45 degree angle or the gravity center. For May Beans these prices are 218 3/8, 240 3/8, 251 7/8 and 319 1/8.

On the weekly or monthly chart, use the date when the extreme high or extreme low is made and draw a 45 degree angle up and down starting from the above half-way points. These angles are very important for determining highs and lows and a change in trend.

From the extreme lows or extreme highs, you add or subtract the proportionate parts of the circle, as given below.

44 added to 360 gives 404. From 404 subtract 90 gives 314, and the degree in the sign is 14 degrees Aquarius. 90 degrees or square from this is 234 or 16 degrees Scorpio.

436 3/4 minus 360 gives 76 3/4 or 16 degrees 45' in the sign Gemini. Subtract 120 gives 16 degrees 45' Aquarius or a price of 316 3/4. A square or 90 degrees from this is 16 degrees 45' Scorpio, price 226 3/4.

The lows of 67, 68 and 69 equal 7, 8 and 9 degrees in Gemini. 120 degrees subtracted gives 307, 308 and 309, the triangle points which are 7, 8 and 9 degrees Aquarius. Subtract 90 degrees from these prices gives 217, 218 and 219 or 7, 8 and 9 degrees in Pisces.

131 high, add 180, gives 311 or 11 degrees Aquarius. Subtract 90 gives 221 or 11 degrees Scorpio.

October 5, 1936, futures trading started in Soy Beans. The first sale was 120. Add 180 gives 300 or 30 degrees in Capricorn.

218 3/8 is 8 degrees 22' Scorpio. Add 90 gives 308 3/8 or 8½ degrees in Aquarius.

240 3/8 is 0 degrees 22' in Sagittarius. Add 60 gives 300 3/8. Add 90 gives 330 3/8.

251 7/8 is 12 degrees in Sagittarius. Add 60 gives 311 7/8 or 12 degrees Aquarius. Add 90 gives 348 or 12 degrees Pisces.

1930, June high 216. Equals 6 degrees Scorpio. Add 90 gives 306 or 6 degrees Aquarius. Add 225 gives 441, which is the square of 21, and 441 is 21 degrees in the sign Gemini, which is 81 more than 360, the square of 9.

436 3/4, subtract 135, gives 201 3/4 or 1 degree 45' Aquarius. Subtract 180

gives 256 3/4 or 16 degrees 45' Sagittarius. Subtract 225 gives 221 3/4 or 1 degree 45' Sagittarius. Subtract 236¼ gives 200¼ or 20 degrees 15 Min. Libra. The low on May Beans in Feb. 1949 was 201½.

344½, subtract 33 3/4 gives 310 3/4 or 10 degrees 45' Aquarius. Subtract 45 gives 299½ or 29 degrees 30' Capricorn.

120, add 90 gives 210 or 30 degrees Scorpio. Add 125 gives 255 or 15 degrees Sagittarius. Add 180 gives 300 or 30 degrees Capricorn.

67, add 90 gives 157 or 7 degrees Virgo. Add 135 gives 202 or 22 degrees Libra. Add 120 gives 127 or 7 degrees Libra. Add 180 gives 247 or 7 degrees Sagittarius. Add 225 gives 292 or 22 degrees Capricorn. Add 240 gives 307 or 7 degrees Aquarius. Add 270 gives 337 or 7 degrees Pisces. Add 315 gives 382 or 22 degrees Aries. Add 360 gives 427 of 7 degrees Gemini. Add 271¼ gives 438¼. High on May beans was 436 3/4. After that high the next extreme low was 201½. Note that 67 plus 125 gives 202, and that one-half of 405 is 202½, and 180 plus 22½ is 202½, which are the mathematical reasons why May Soy Beans made bottom at 201½.

All of the above price levels can be measured in Time Periods of days, weeks and months, and when the time periods come out at these prices, it is important for a change in trend, especially if confirmed by the geometrical angles from highs and lows.

ACTIVE ANGLES AND DEGREES

By live or active angles is meant Prices and Time Periods where the Longitude of the major planets are or where the squares, triangles, oppositions are to these planets.

The averages of the six major planets Heliocentric and Geocentric are the most powerful points for Time and Price resistance. Also the Geocentric and Heliocentric average of the five major planets with Mars left out, is of great importance and should be watched.

You should also calculate the averages of eight planets which move around the Sun as this is the first most important odd square. The square of "1" is one, and "1" is the Sun. 8 added to "1" gives 9, the square of 3 and completes the first important odd square, which is important for Time and Price.

Examples of live, active angles: At the present writing, Jan. 18, 1954, Saturn Geo. is 8 to 9 degrees Scorpio. Add the square or 90 degrees gives 8 to 9 degrees Aquarius and equals the price 309-309, for May Beans.
The planet Jupiter is at 21 degrees Gemini, which is 81 degrees in longitude from "0" the square of 9. Subtract 135 degrees from Jupiter gives 306 or 6 degrees Aquarius. This is why Soy Beans have met resistance so many times between 306 and 311¼. The Price Resistance levels come out strong around these degrees and prices and the Geometrical angles come out on daily, weekly and monthly, but the power of Saturn and Jupiter aspects, working out Time to these Price Resistance Levels, is what halts the advance in Soy Beans.

24 Revolutions of Time and Price The earth makes one revolution on its axis in 24 hours, moving 360 degrees in Longitude. One hour of Time equals 15 degrees in Longitude, and for one hour of Time, we use one cent of Price. This is for daily active markets but can be used for weekly and monthly time periods, as

you can see by the Master Charts.

The Longitude of the Planets and the Longitude of the average of the planets determine the Resistance Levels as the price moves around each cycle of 24 cents per bushel. You mark on the Master Chart all low prices with a red circle around them and place around all high prices a green circle. Then note the Angles of 45, 60, 90, 120, 135, 180, 225, 240, 270, 300, 315 and 260 from each high and low. Then check the Longitude of the Planets and the Longitude of the average of the planets to see when the Price reaches these degrees or aspects and meets resistance.

Example: Dec. 2, 1953, May Soy Beans high 311¼. This equalled 18 degrees 45' in Pisces, close square or 90 degrees of Jupiter, 135 degrees to Saturn and 180 degrees of the averages, and 120 degrees of Uranus.

300 price equals 30 degrees Virgo. 302 equals 30 degrees Libra. 304 equals 30 degrees Scorpio. On Jan. 18, 1954, the planet Saturn Geo. is 8 degrees 30' Scorpio, and 15 degrees Scorpio gives a price of 303, therefore when May Beans decline to 302, they will be below the body or longitude of Saturn and will indicate lower. At the same time, using the Earth's annual revolution of 365¼ days to move around the Sun, a price of 308½ is 90 degrees or square to Saturn. As long as the price is below 308½ it is within the square and in position to go lower. But by the 24 revolution, when the price breaks below 304, it is in the bear sign Scorpio, a fixed sign and will indicate lower prices.

Study and analyze all options of all commodities in the same way as we have analyzed May Beans. Remember, when these Resistance Points are met you must give the market time to show that it is making tops or bottoms and getting ready to make a change in trend. Do not guess, wait until you get a definite indication of a change in trend before deciding that the main trend has changed. You can buy or sell agianst these resistance levels and place a stop loss order. Having before you all the information outlined above, you would certainly have gone short of May Soy Beans on Dec. 2, 1953 and cover your shorts on Dec. 17 at 296 because the price was down to the 45 degree angle from 44 on the Monthly high and low chart.

24 CENT MOVES OR MORE

It is very important to watch the action on the daily and weekly chart when the price is up or down 24 cents from any high or low, 48 cents, 72 cents most important because three times 24, 96 cents, 120 or 5 times 24; 144 of great importance because 6 times 24 and the square of 12, 168 which is 7 times 24 - very important. You can also use one-half of 24, which is 12, and watch 36, 60, 84, etc. which equals 180 degrees or half the circle or cycle.

CHAPTER 4

MAY COFFEE SANTOS D

HELIOCENTRIC AND GEOCENTRIC ASPECTS AND PLANETS

MAY COFFEE SANTOS D
March 19, 1954
High 8729

Using a scale of one point to one degree, 8729 equals 29° Gemini.
Using a scale of 30 points to one degree, equals 21° Capricorn.
Using the Jupiter scale of 12 points to one degree, equals 7° 30' Aries.
Using one cent to one degree, equals 27° 16' Gemini.

The dollar value is $28,171.00, which equals 11° 45' Capricorn.
The average price of 5 options on March 19, 1954 was 8663, which equals 28° Aries, or 60° from the Heliocentric Jupiter. Heliocentric Jupiter is 20° 35' Gemini, which means that the price of 8729 was at this degree. Heliocentric Uranus is 21° 52' Cancer and the price at 21° Capricorn is opposite to this.

April 16, 1954 is 276 months from April 16, 1931, low 435. Using 50 points per month, the 45° angle crossed 8715 on March 19, 1954, and the Sun has moved 8253 degrees from April 16, 1931. Add this to 435 gives 8688 as the resistance angle.

MARCH COFFEE - October 1, 1936 low 300. Time to April 1, 1954 210 months at 30 points per month, the 45° angle crosses at 5600, and at 40 points per months, it crosses at 8700.

1931, April 16 to March 19, 1954 - Geocentric Saturn moved 285° 38'. This would give a price of 8572. 1936, October 1 to March 19, 1954 - Geocentric Saturn moved 231° , which would equal a price of 7230.

1940, May 15 to March 19, 1954 - Saturn moved 181° 35', which gives a price of 6990 and using 45 points to one degree would give 8715.

1940, August 19 - Saturn moved 173° 23'. At 45 points to one degree, this equals 8760 price.

HELIOCENTRIC SATURN - 1931, April 16 to March 19, 1954, Saturn moved 287° 15' which equals 17° 13' Capricorn, price 8632.

1936, October 1, Saturn moved 225°, which gives a price of 7150.

1940, May 15, Saturn gained 179° 44', price 5940.
1940, August 19, Saturn gained 176° 14', price 5842.

HELIOCENTRIC PLANETS, March 19, 1954

Jupiter 89° 35' equals 29° 35' Gemini.
Saturn 214.44 equals 4° 44' Scorpio
Uranus 111.52 equals 21° 52' Cancer

The average of these 6 planets is 164.17 or 14° 17' Virgo.

GEOCENTRIC PLANETS

Neptune 204.35 equals 24° 35' Libra
Pluto 144 equals 24° Leo
Mars 221 equals 11° Scorpio

The average of the 6 Geocentric planets is 173.26 or 25° 26' Virgo

One-half of Jupiter to Saturn Helio is 152.09 or 2° 9' Virgo. The average of Saturn, Jupiter, Uranus and Neptune is 155.10, equals 5° 10' Virgo. ½ of this average is 17° 35' Gemini. Jupiter, Uranus ½ is 100.43, equals 10° 43' Cancer Heliocentric. ½ of Geocentric Jupiter to Uranus is 93.48 or 3° 48' Cancer.

IMPORTANT DATES EACH MONTH - 1st, 15th, 18th and 19th. The present market is running close to these dates.

1953, June 19 - May Coffee low 5050
August 17 - high 5765
Sept. 21 - high 5710
Oct. 19 - High 5660

July 17, low 5555
Sept. 15 - low 5565
Oct. 9 - Last low 5470
Dec. 9 - High 6240

1954, Jan. 13 - High 7470
March 15 - High 5625
March 18 - Low 5465

Jan. 19 - Low 6560 - This was 7 months from June 19.
March 19 - High 8729 - This extreme high was 9 months from June 19, low, 2 months from Jan. 19 low, 6 months from Sept. 15, 1953 low and 5 months from Oct. 19 high at 5860.

HELIOCENTRIC & GEOCENTRIC ASPECTS

1954, March 24 - Heliocentric Jupiter enters Cancer.
June 24 - " " 120° of Saturn.
April 12 - Sun 60° of Jupiter Geocentric.
April 15 - Sun 180 of Neptune "
April 13 - Jupiter 135° of Saturn "
April 16 - Jupiter 60 of Pluto "
April 26 - Jupiter 120 of Neptune "
April 26 - Sun 180 of Saturn "

The month of April is very important. There should be great activity and wide swings in prices due to these aspects.

GEOCENTRIC MAPS MOVEMENTS from low prices on Coffee--

1931, April 16 to August 7, 1953 - Mars has made 12 round trips.
1954, October 29 - Mars will be opposite or 180° from its place on April 16, 1931.

1936, October 1 to September 19, 1953 - Mars made 9 round trips of 360° each.
1954, Dec. 9 - Mars will be 9½ round trips or opposite its place Oct. 1, 1936.

1940, May 15 to June 12, 1953 - Mars made 7 round trips or complete cycles.
1954, Apr. 9 - Mars is 7½ cycles or opposite its place on May 15, 1940. Due to the retrograde position of Mars, it will again be 7½ on July 7 and on Aug. 17, 1954 or the third time in opposition to its own place, which is very important.

1940, August 19 to Sept. 15, 1953 - Mars had completed 7 round trips. Note low on Coffee on that date.
1954, Dec. 4 - Mars 7½ round trips or opposite its own place on Aug. 19, 1940.

If Coffee starts to decline between March 22 and 24, 1954, it should continue down to around April 15, when the adverse aspects of Jupiter to Saturn and the Sun to Neptune are completed. From these dates, you should watch for the possibility of a rally up to April 16, 1954, when Jupiter is 120 of Neptune and the Sun 130 of Saturn. This might cause a quick rally followed by a sharp quick decline. By studying all of the data outlined above and applying it to Coffee, you will be able to learn more about what causes the changes in trend.

March 20, 1954

W. D. GANN

Apply the same rules to grains or any other commodity and by study and practice you will learn how to determine a change in trend from a strong to a weak position to a strong position.

Remember that you have signed an agreement not to reveal these rules and instructions to anyone, and by keeping these secret discoveries confidential for your own use, you will later receive the very important CE AVERAGE, and the MOF FORMULA which is only taught to students who have taken the same course as you have and we do not reveal it to students who take the minor courses and pay less money.

Wishing you success, I am

Yours very truly,

November 6, 1954

GANN'S Coffee Horoscope

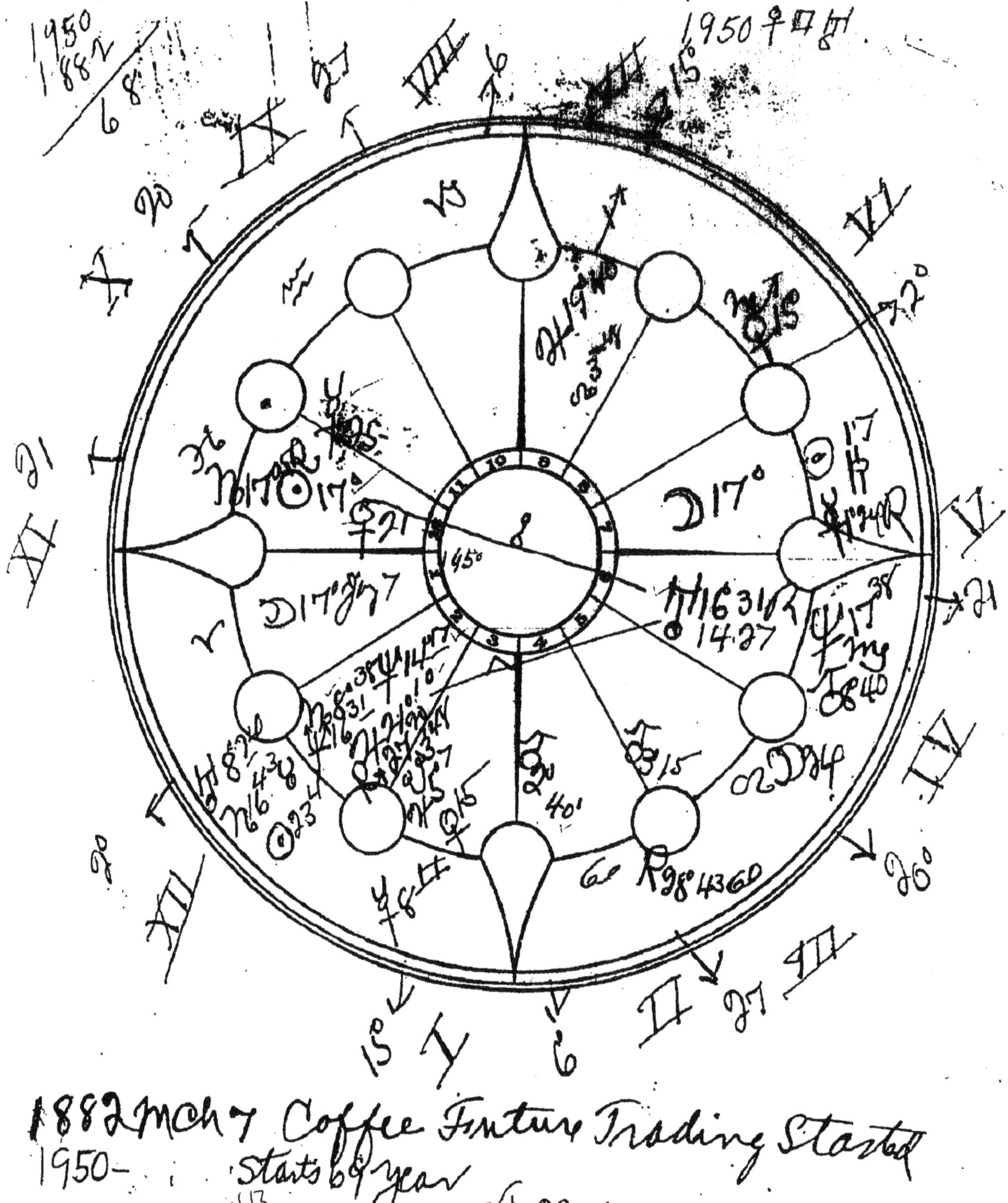

1882 Mch 7 Coffee Futur Trading Started

1950- Starts 69 year

Sept 28 1936 10 30 AM

S.T. 23.01
1.30
21.31

Oct 10-1936
Low 34

2/8

1/8

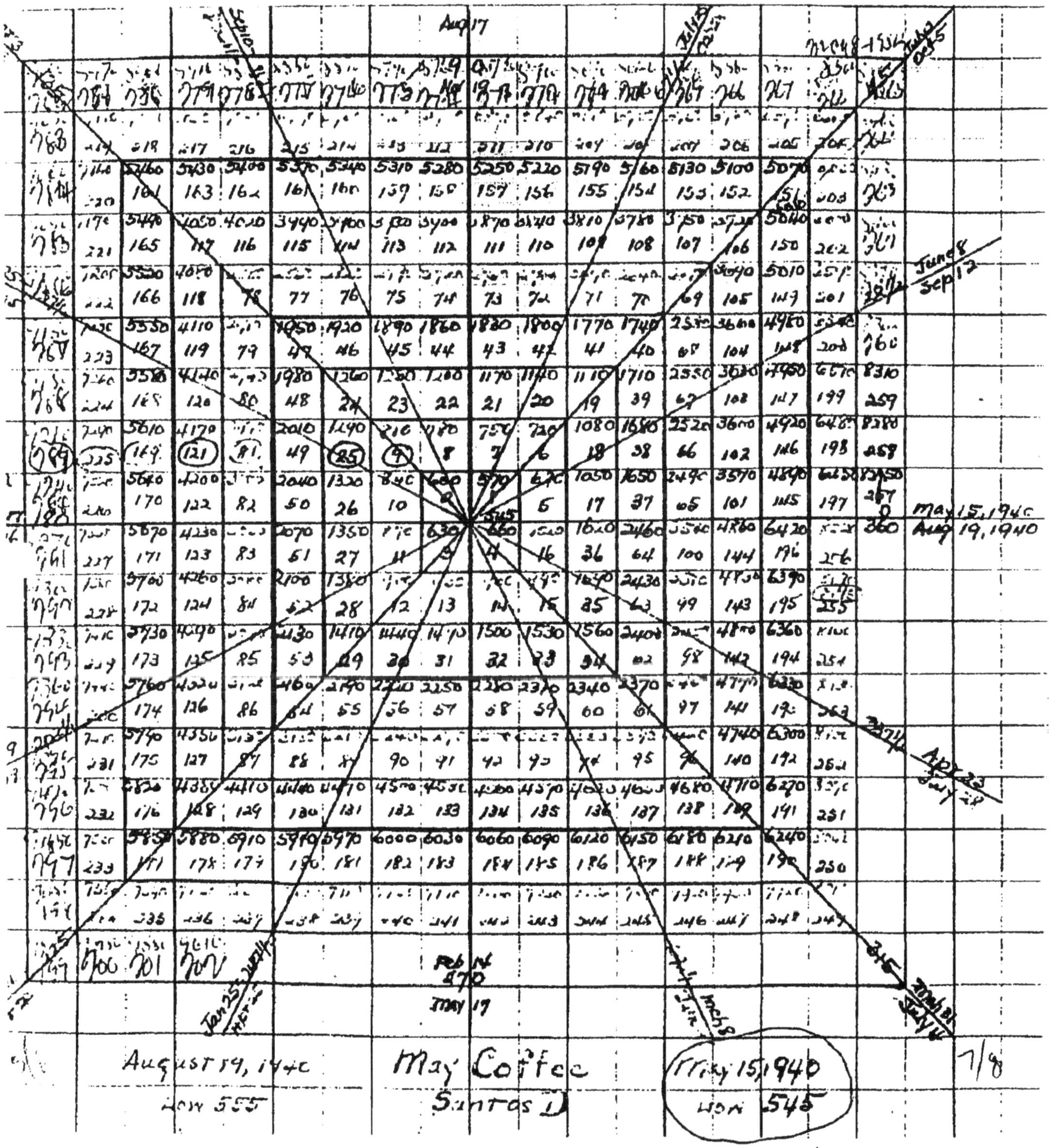

7/8

August 19, 1940

Low 555

May Coffee

Santos D

May 15, 1940

Low 545

6/8

545 (2) ∅ or 540

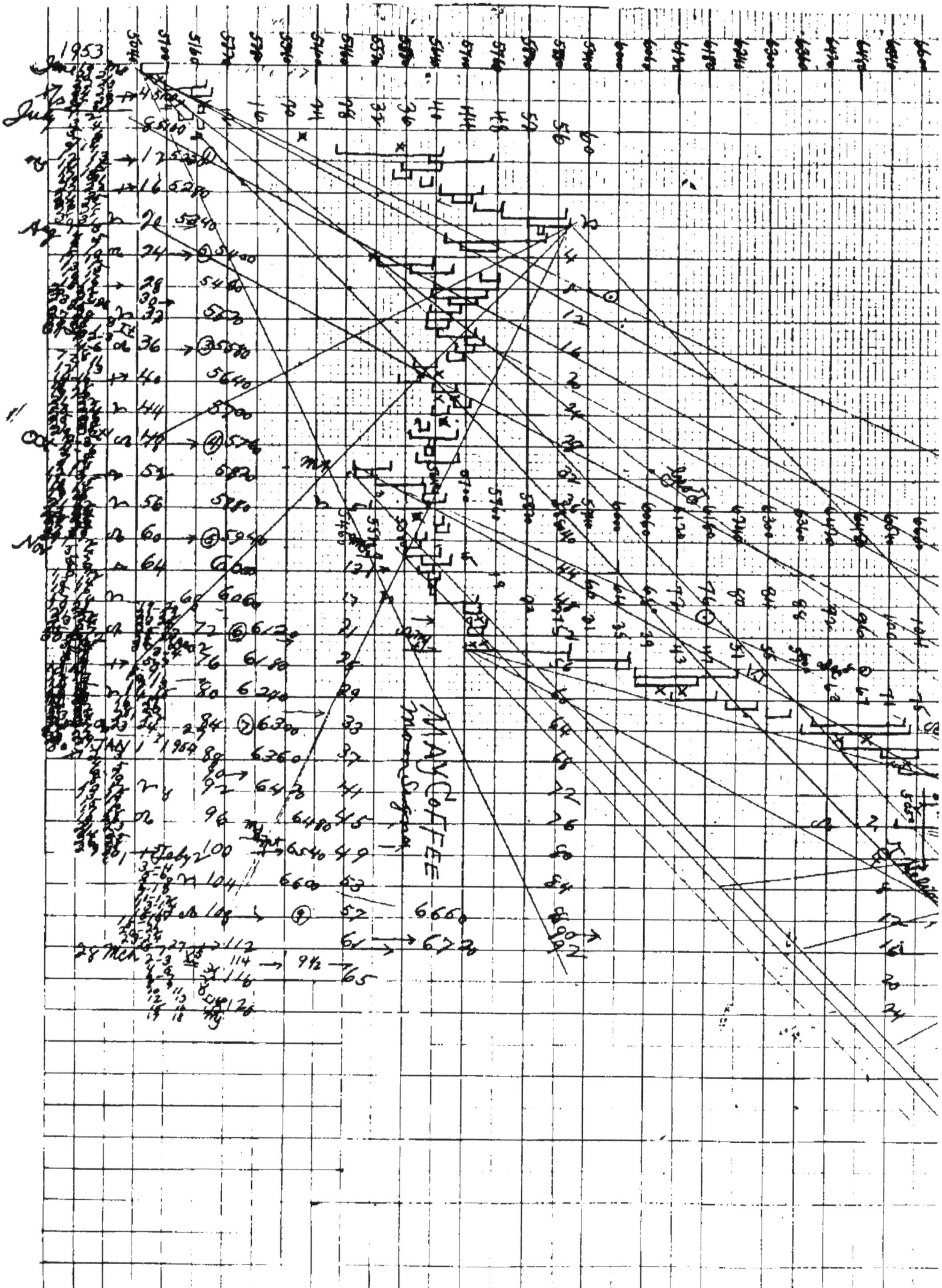
1953
MAY COFFEE

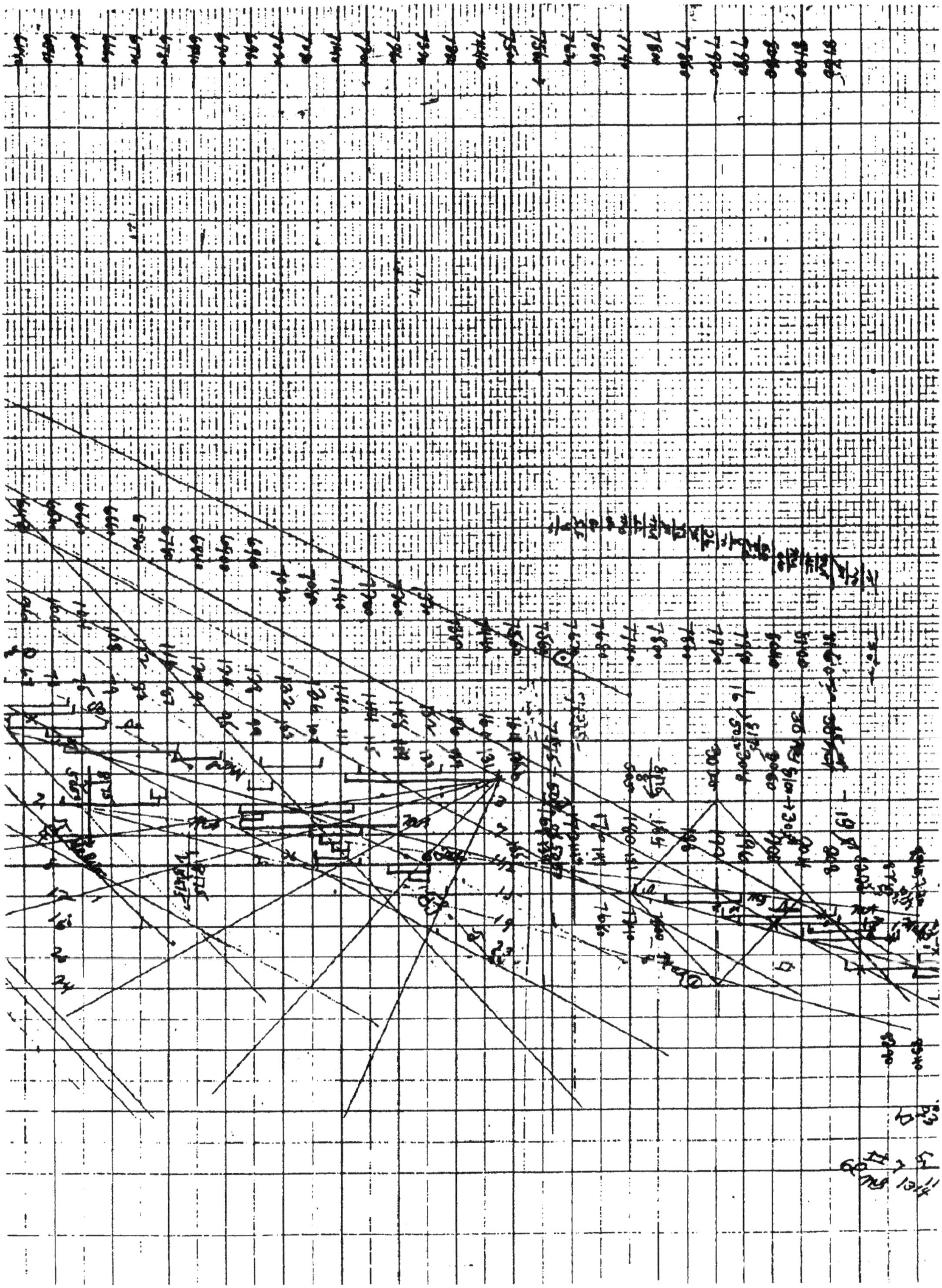

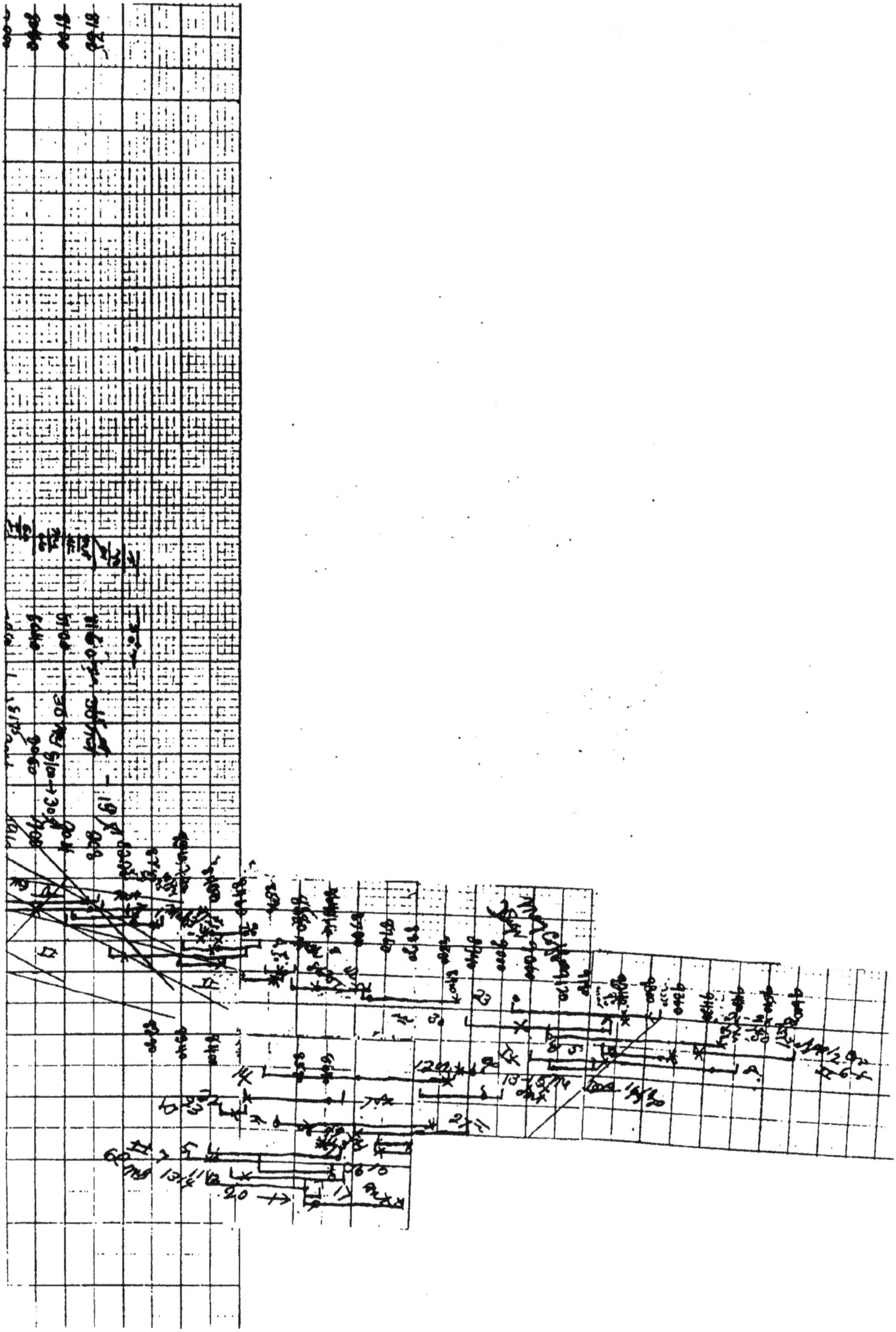

MASTER TIME & PRICE CHART
PLOTTING OF OPPOSIT POINTS

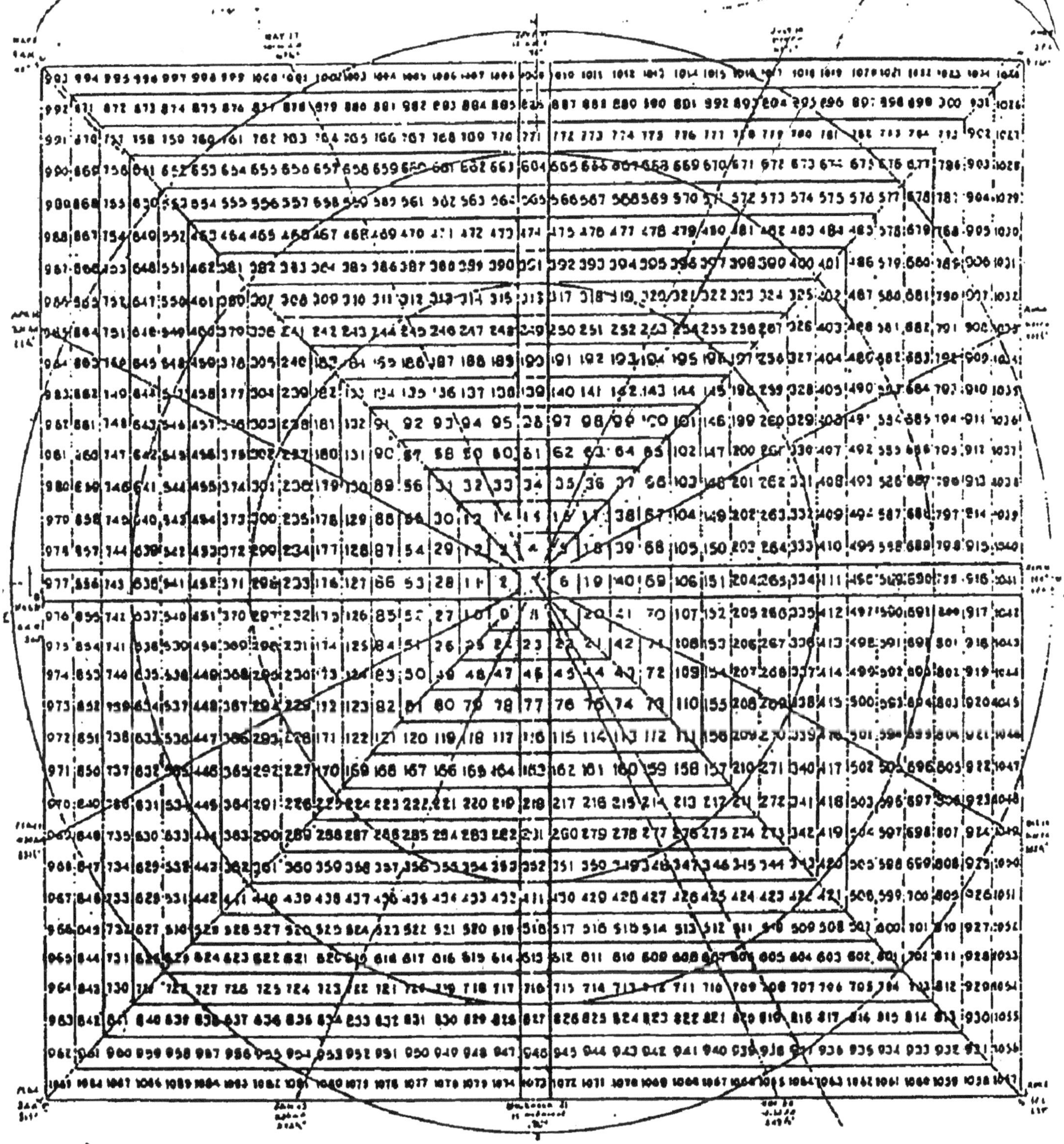

PRICES OR TIME ON ORANGE LINES ARE ACTUAL
OR UNNATURAL PRICES OPP. C TIME
TIME ON ORANGE LINES ARE TURNING POINTS.

CHAPTER 5

ASTROLOGICAL CHARTS AND TABLES

1	44 = 22° 26		28	014 3/4 = 28° 36	
2	67	26° ♍	29	320 1/2 = 14° ♉	
3	68 1/2	8° ♎ ①	30	328 1/2	8° II
4	69	12 " ④	31	334	20 ♍
5	120	30 ♐	32	344 1/2	26° ♐
6	131 1/2	2° 26	33	361	8° ♈ ⑤
7	154 1/2	6° ♍	34	422	16° ♌ ④
8	164	22° ♐	35	425	10° ♍
9	182 1/2	4° ♈ ①	36	486 3/4	14° ♐
10	201 1/2	24° ♍	37	405	30° 26
11	207	28° "			
12	203	6° ♎ ③			
13	0	30° ♐			
14	220 1/2	4° ♐			
15	224	22° 26			
16	232 1/2	30° ♉			
17	235 1/2	26° 60			
18	285	22° 60			
19	276 3/4	24° ♉			
20	265 3/4	28° ♒ ②			
21	268 1/4	16° 26			
22	279 3/4	18° II			
23	281	28° II			
24	255	22° ♐			
25	[illegible] 306 1/2	24° ♑			
26	[illegible] 305	17° ♒ ③			
27	309 3/4	18° ♐ ④			

670 – 6
☍ 6 13
☌ 6
□ 5 > 9
△ 8
✶ 7 17
30° 4
150 5

☌	☍	60	120		
26° ♍	6	60	♐	♑	♉
6	24	26	30	24°	30°
24	2	22	22°	①	24
28	22	②	30		14
2	16		22		③
10	28		26°		
⑤	30		⑤		
	⑥ ☍				

♈	♌	♐	II	♒	♒
4°	16	4°	18	8	28
8		14°	28	6	12
2	1	2	8		18
			3	②	3
			5 □	5	

Mean of 5 MOE – Mars out of 8 – CE

O of 8 – Cycle of Eight

♄ Scale of Cycle

	♈	♉	♊	♋	♌	♍	♈	♉	♊	♋	♌	♍	
30	900	1800	2700	3600	4500		2530	5040	7560	10080	15120	17640	
28	840	1740	2640	3540	4440		2436						
24	720	1620	2520	3420	4320		2100	4536					
20	600	1500	2400	3300	4200		1680						
16	480	1380	2280	3180	4080								
		1350	2176	3090			1260	3780				15	1.890.00 Aug
12	360	1260	2160	3060	3960								15 ♎
							840	3360				10	184°20
8	240	1140	2040	2940	3840		756	3276					
4	120	1020	1920	2820	3720		420	2940					
			1830		3330	4530							
0	0 ♈	900 ♉	1800 ♊	2700 ♋	3600 ♌	4500 ♍	0 ♈	2520	5040 ♊	7560 ♋	10080	15120	17640 ♎

♃ Scale of Cycle

	♈ 1	♉ 2	♊ 3	♋ 4	♌ 5	♍ 6	♎ 7	♏ 8	♐ 9	♑ 10	♒ 11	♓ 12	
30	360	720	1080	1440	1800	2160	2520	2880	3240	3600	3960	4320	
	348	708	1068	1428		2148	2508	2868	3228	3588	3948	4308	
28	336	696	1056	1416	1776	2136	2496	2856	3216	3576	3936	4296	
24	288	648	1008	1368	[illegible]	2088	2448	2808	3168	3528	3888	4248	
20	240	600	960	1320	1680	2040	2400	2760	3120	3480	3840	4200	
16	192	552	912	1272	1632	1992	2352	2712	3072	3432	3792	4152	
	180	540	900	1260	1620	1980	2340	2700	3060	3420	3780	4140	
12	144	504	864	1224	1584	1944	2304	2664	3024	3384	3744	4104	
8	96	456	816	1176	1536	1896	2256	2596	2976	3336	3696	4056	
4	48	408	768	1128	1488	1848	2208	2548	2928	3288	3648	4008	1.890 = 3°30' ♏
0	♈	360 ♉	720 ♊	1080 ♋	1440 ♌	1800 ♍	♎	♏	2880 ♐	3240 ♑	3600 ♒	3960 ♓	

♃ Jupiter Scale of cycle

☉ 15° in 15 Days 30 = 30 A

♃ 7½ 15° " 15 " 30 "

1932 June 9 ♂ Helio 31° 30 = 1° 30 ♂ (Correction written above) 28 / 12 / 40

1934 May (1)
1936 Ap (2)
1938 Feby (3)
1940 Dec (4)
1941 Nov (5)
1943 Oct (6)
1945 Aug (7)
1947 July 8
1949 June (9)
1951 Apr (10) — Inner 360 — 3600
1952 May 3 = 11.30 m
1 30
10.00 —

1938 Dec 10 ♂ H 182 = 2° [illegible] =		
1940 Nov		
1942 Oct	2	36
1944 Aug	2	72
1946 July	3	108°
1948 May	4	144° — 1440
1950 Apr	5	180
1952 Mch 8 — 2° [illegible]	6	216°
	7	360

May 3 — 12 m → 252°
4°
256°

1440
777
2167

190° — 190 777 = 3287
379° 3287

May 3 Helio ♂ at 379°

1951 Mch 8 ♂ 17° 30 [illegible] = 330 at 1° 30 [illegible]
1 30 — 16 — 3240
16 00 — 346 — 346
3586

Mch 8 — 1951 — ♂ at → 3586

1951 Nov 9 ♂ 142° = 2° [illegible] or 3600 + 90 = 3690

Average 6 Helio Planets Gain about 3° per

76 - 1st = 60° to 1 Point Prec or Time
2 912 - 30°
3 918 - 20°
4 924 - 15
5 930 - 12°
6 936 - 10°
7 942 8½
8 948 - 7½
9 954 - 6½
10 60 6°
11 66 - 5½
12 72 - 5 — 397 - 5° or 403 - 5°
13 78 - 4½ 98 10 404 10
4 84 4° 99 15 405 15
15 90 4 400 20 406 20
16 96 3° 40 1 25 407 25
17 102 3½ 2 30° 408 30
18 108 - 3° 25
19 114 - 3° 10
120 or 3° to 1 pt

0 = 6 Gain 6
7 9 8
7 = ½ Day 7) 14 / 7

47) 360 / 336 / 24

47) 360 (7 / 336 / 24

54) 360 (6 / 324 / 26

66) 360 (5 / 330 / 30

360 3 / 312 / 42

102) 360 (3 / 306 / 54

108 / 3 / 324

36 / 114 / 3 / 342

342

18 / 18) 144 (8 / 144

Table for Eggs
1° = 5 points
30° 1 Sign = 150 points
⊙ ☽ 1800 points ⊙ = 360

Degrees / Sign		⊙	☽	
360 ♓	[illegible]	3600 … 3500	5400 … [illegible]	1800 … [illegible]
330 ♒	[illegible]	3450	[illegible]	1650
300 ♑	[illegible]	3300 … 3200	5100 … 5000	1500 … [illegible]
270 ♐	[illegible]	[illegible]	[illegible]	[illegible]
240 ♏	[illegible]	3000 … [illegible]	[illegible] … 4700	[illegible]
210 ♎	[illegible]	[illegible]	[illegible]	[illegible]
180 ♍	[illegible]	[illegible] … 2600	[illegible] … 4400	[illegible]
150 ♌	[illegible]	[illegible]	[illegible]	[illegible]
120 ♋	[illegible]	[illegible]	[illegible]	600 … 550
90 ♊	[illegible]	[illegible]	[illegible]	[illegible]
60 ♉	[illegible]	[illegible]	[illegible]	[illegible]
30 ♈	[illegible]	[illegible] … 1800	[illegible]	[illegible]

Note how GANN is using the minimum fluctuation to set up a zodiac relationship with price. This is what he is doing in the coffee letter.

USA (GANN'S GREAT Mutations Chart

Declaration of Independence & Columbus Discovers America

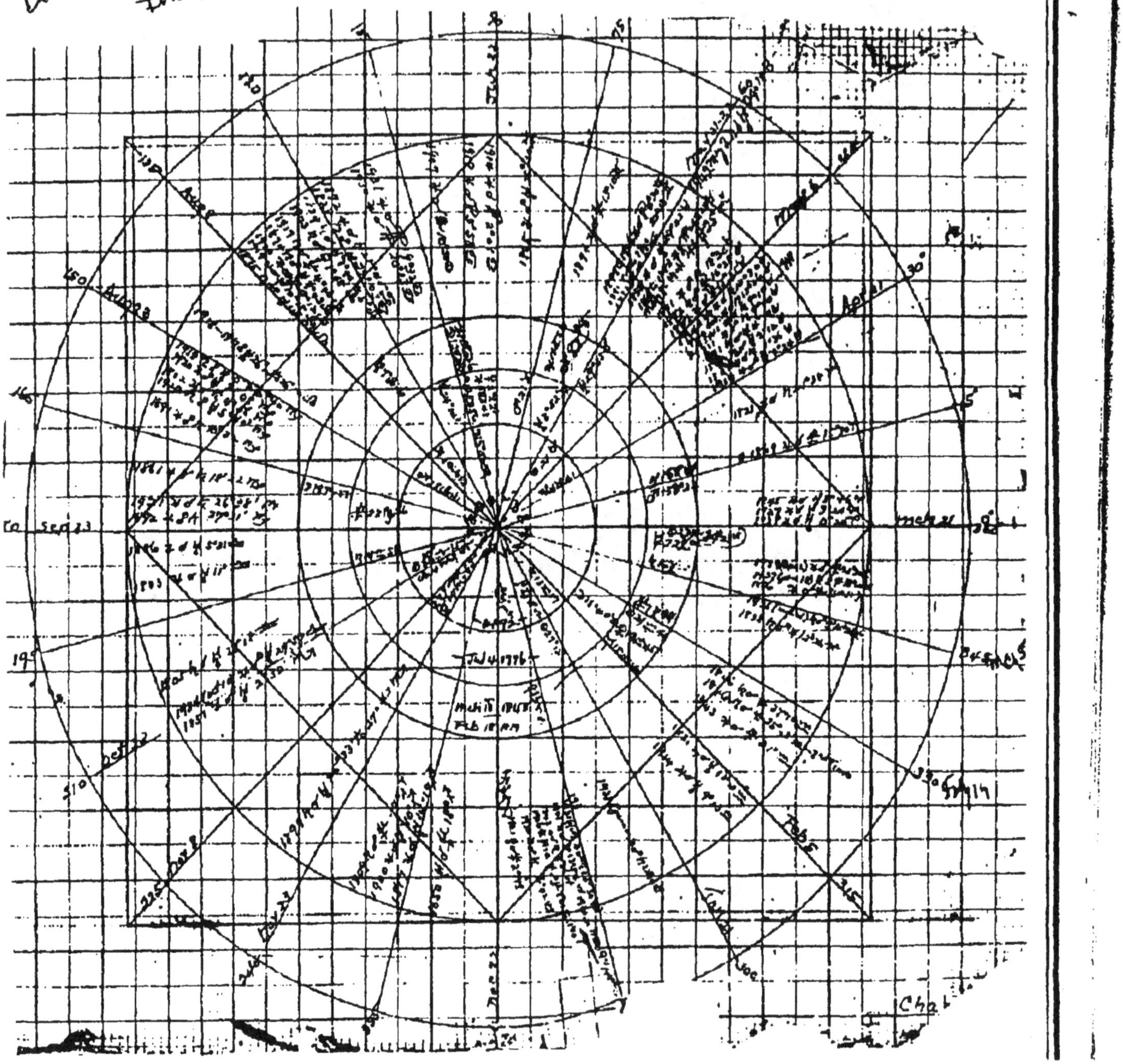

Soybeans (GANN'S Great Mutations Chart)

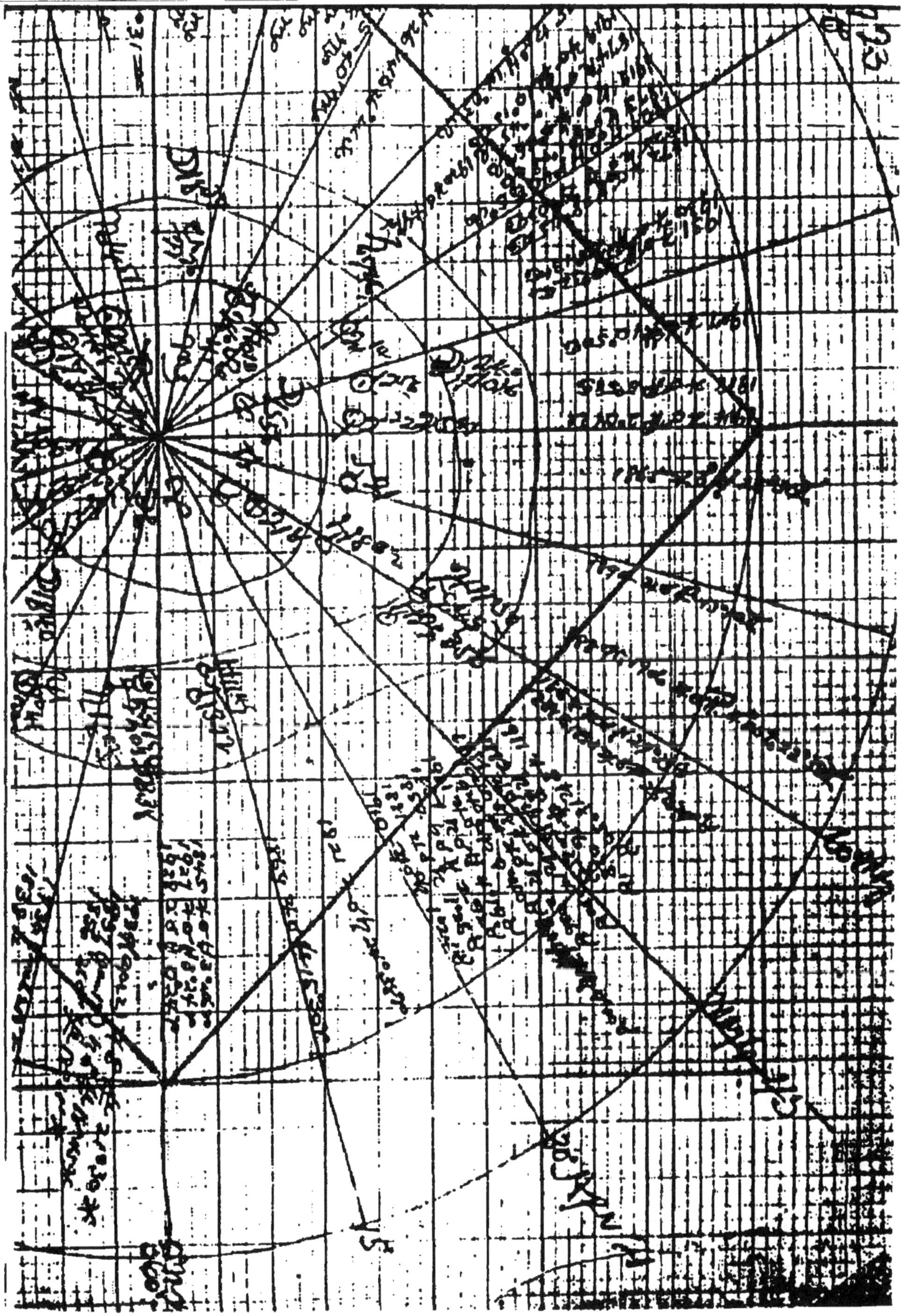

ORIGINAL CIRCLE chart

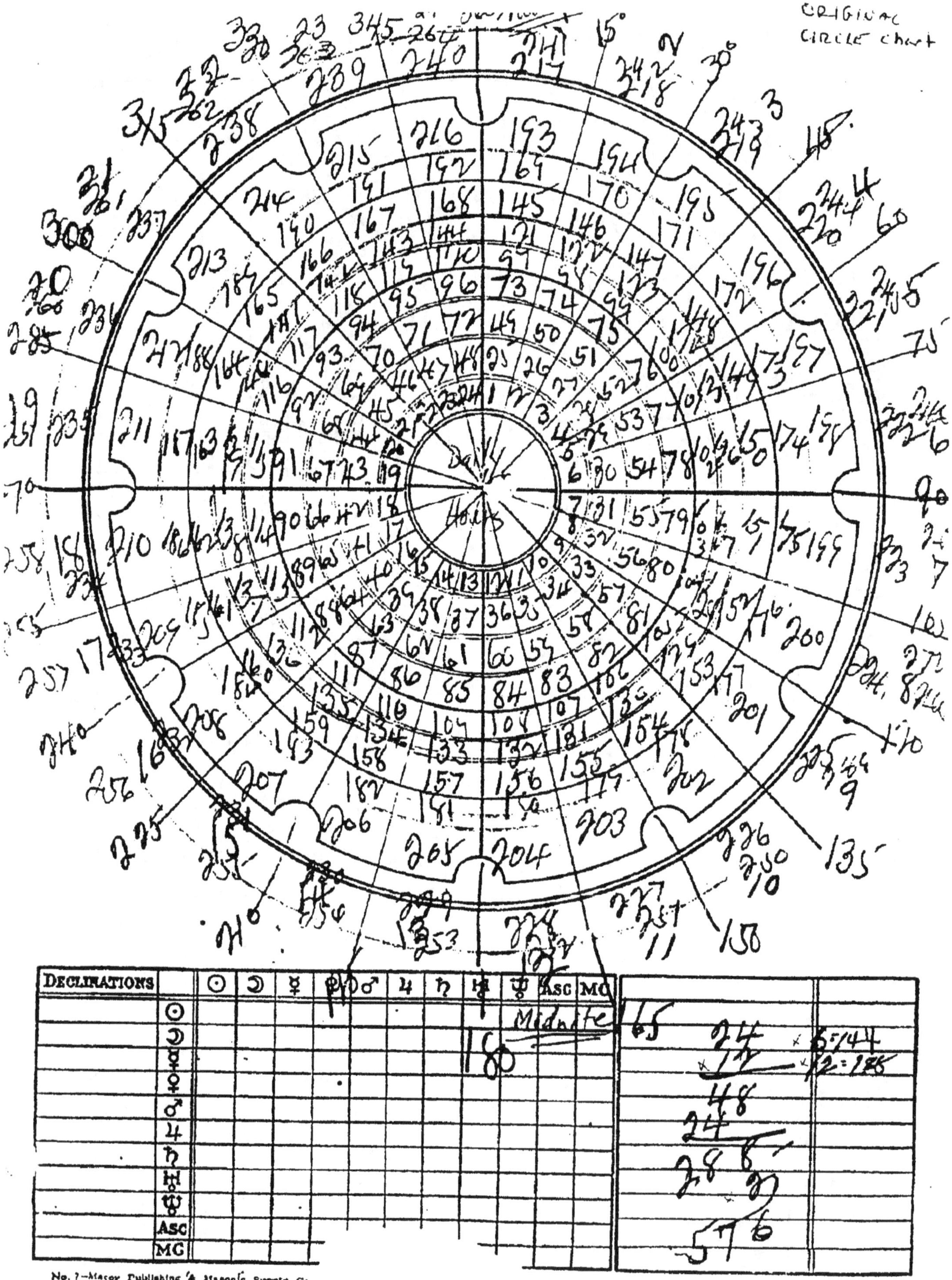

DECLINATIONS		☉	☽	☿	♀	♂	♃	♄	♅	♆	ASC	MC
	☉									Midnite		
	☽								180			
	☿											
	♀											
	♂											
	♃											
	♄											
	♅											
	♆											
	ASC											
	MC											

165

24 × 5:144
× 12 = 188
48
24
288
576

No. 7—Macoy Publishing & Masonic Supply Co

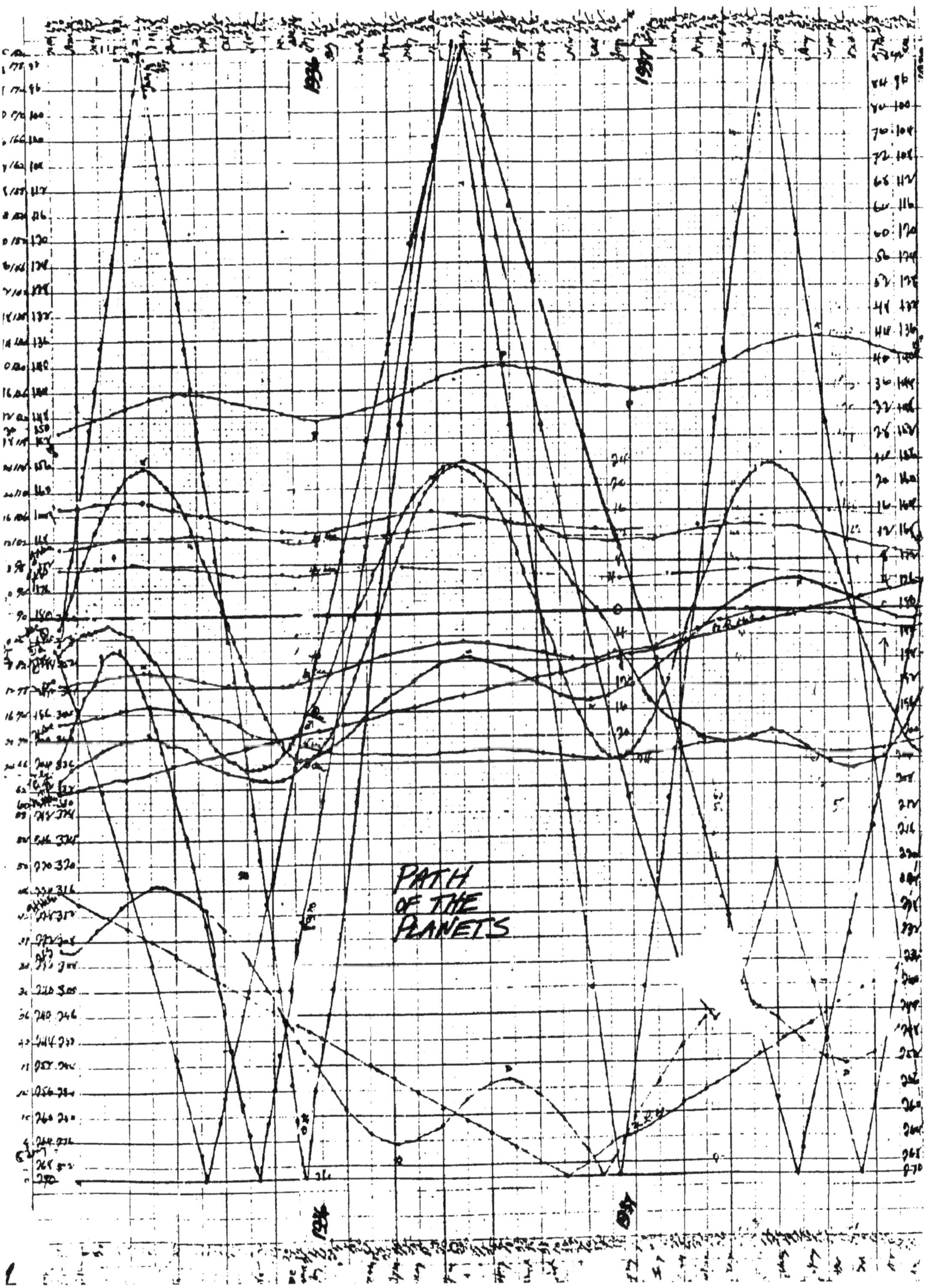
PATH
OF THE
PLANETS

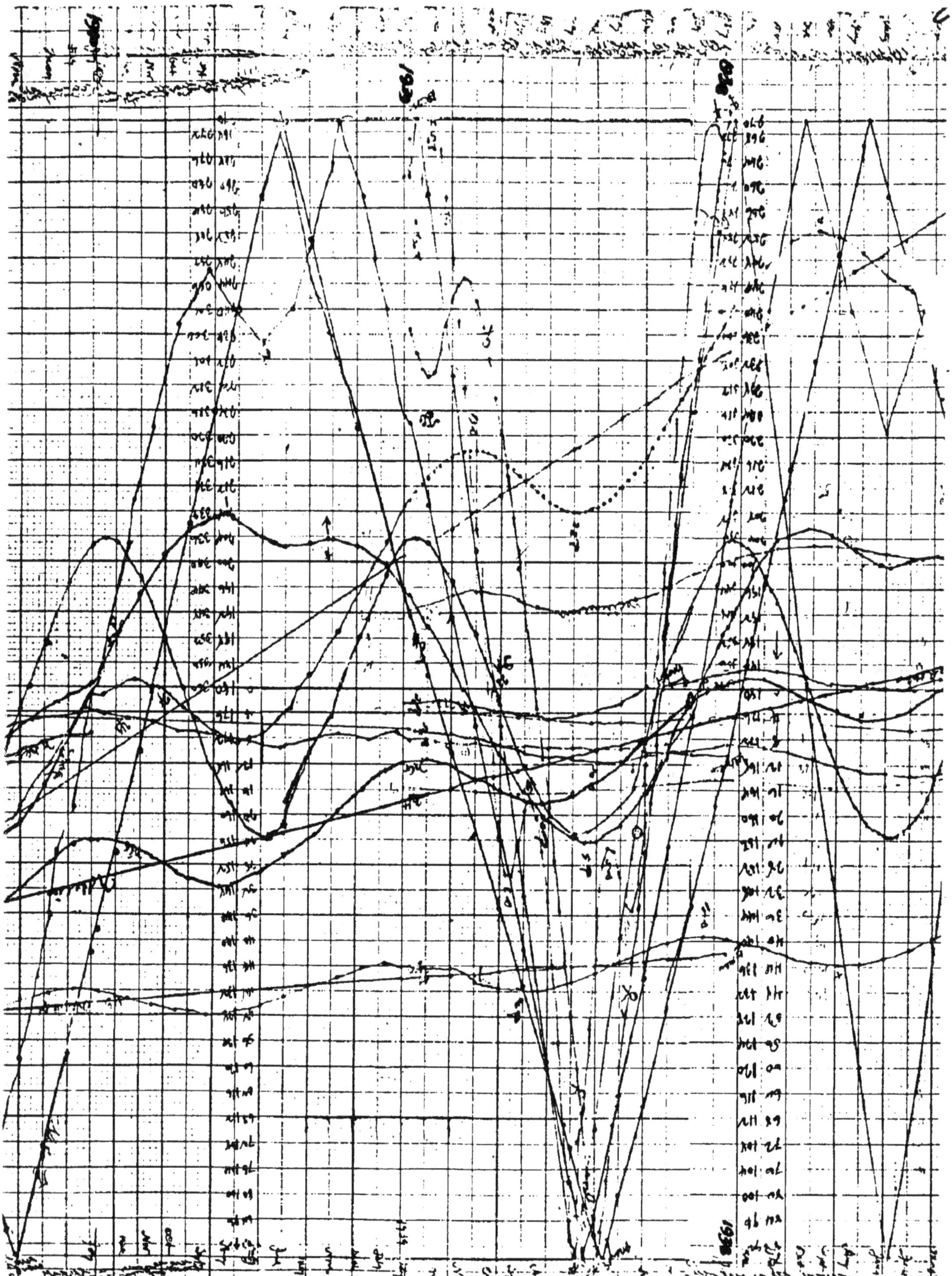

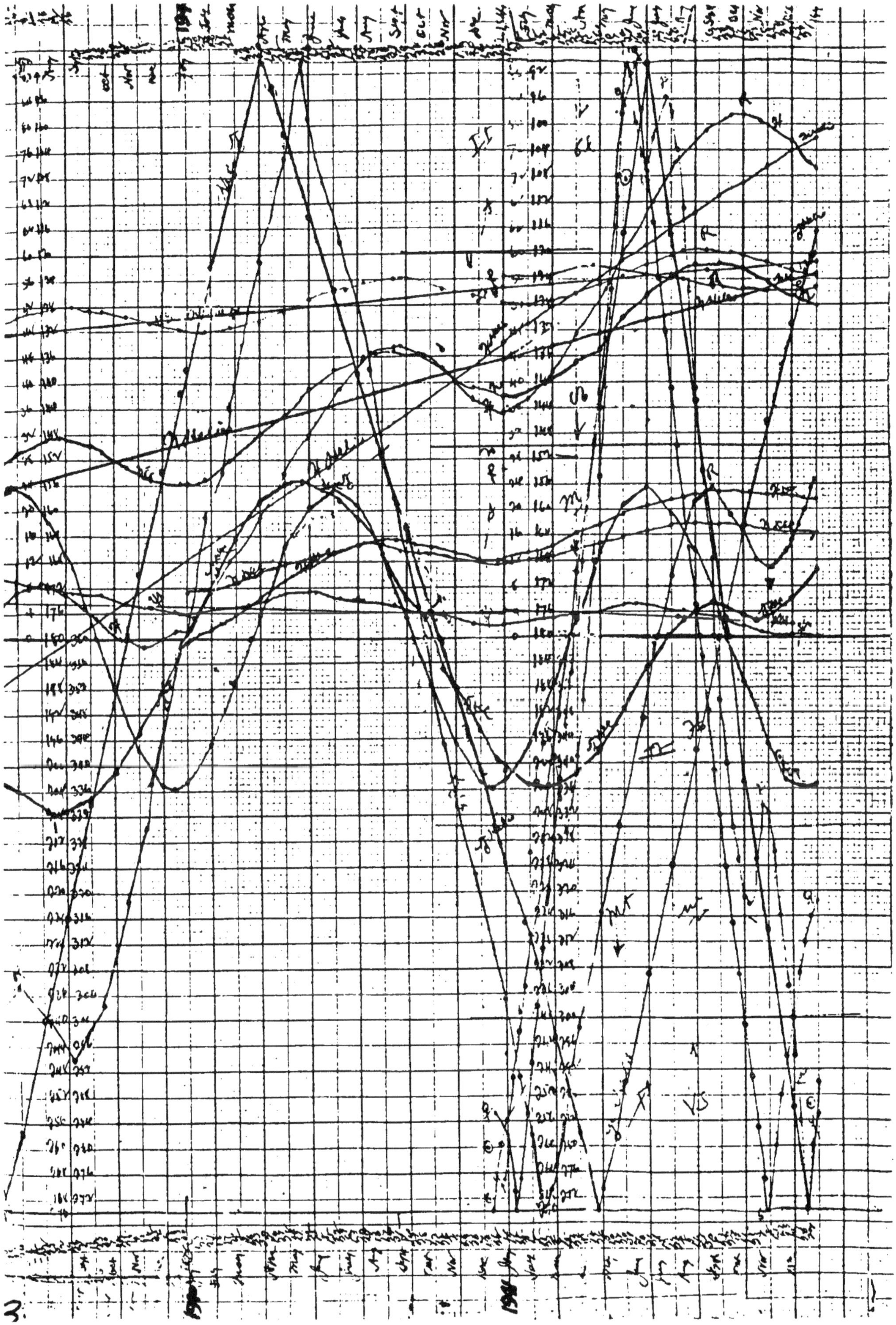

3.

COSMOLOGICAL ECONOMICS

THE MASTERS OF FINANCIAL ASTROLOGY SERIES

The Masters of Financial Astrology Series brings together a collection of the most important classical and modern works on Astroeconomics or astrological financial market forecasting. These classic works written from the Golden Age of Technical Analysis to current times were carefully selected by the late Dr. Jerome Baumring of the Investment Centre Bookstore in the 1980's, as representing the most valuable and important works in financial astrology ever written. They were included as the foundational source texts for his program in advanced financial market analysis and forecasting, and serve as the ideal foundation for any analyst seeking a thorough education in astrological applications to financial market theory and forecasting.

The Golden Age of technical analysis was a period from the early 1900's through the 1960's where the foundational theories of modern financial analysis and financial astrology came into full form. The ideas and technologies developed during this fruitful period include the first serious research into the modern field of Astro-Economics, or Financial Astrology and related fields like cycle analysis, cosmic causation, solar influence on geomagnetic and Earthly events like weather, earthquakes, climate change and radio disturbance. Though financial astrology is actually a subject that stretches back centuries, if not millennia, this ripe period saw the real advent of popular research and theoretical development of this vast study of the interaction between cosmic forces and Earthly phenomena. This collection represents the best work available within this field.

Each quality reprint of these classical texts has been reproduced as an exact facsimile of the original text, maintaining the original layout, typeset, charts, and style of the author and time period, helping to preserve and communicate a sense of the feeling of the original work that a reproduction in modern format does not capture. Many of these rare works and courses were originally printed in only very small private editions or as correspondence courses, so that the originals were easily lost or destroyed over time. Our reproductions of these important source works are printed on acid free paper and bound in a quality hardcover that will compliment any trading library and help to preserve this important resource for generations to come.

The series is also currently being digitized and archived for permanent digital preservation by the Institute of Cosmological Economics, creating a searchable reference library of market wisdom accessible globally and available in new digital formats to keep the knowledge fresh and accessible through new devices and technology as we advance further into the information revolution. To see our full catalog of hardcover reprints, new publications, and digital editions please visit our website at www.CosmoEconomics.com.

- **Professor Weston** - Forecasting The New York Stock Market - *A Treatise on the Geometrical or Chart System of Forecasting* - (1921)
- **Louise McWhirter** - The McWhirter Theory Of Stock Market Forecasting - *The Theory & Application of Forecasting Trends & Cycles* - (1938)
- **James Mars Langham** - Planetary Effects On Stock Market Prices - *The Effects & Applications of Planetary Positions & Aspects on Prices* - (1932)
- **James Mars Langham** - Cyclical Market Forecasting Stocks & Grains - A Complete Course of Instruction in an Original & Proven System - (1938)
- **Fakir Chandra Dutt** - Market Forecasting - *A Scientific Exposition Of The Influences Of The Heavenly Bodies On The Fluctuations Of Values* - (1949)
- **Richard Scott** - The Planetary Market Barometer – *Trading Stocks, Futures & Forex With Celestial Mechanics* - (2015)
- **Fred White, Professor Weston, W. D. Gann, Sepharial** - The Earliest Financial Astrology Manuscripts - *The Original Works of The Old Masters* - (1902)
- **Donald Bradley** - Stock Market Prediction - *The Historical & Future Siderograph Charts & Software* - (1948)
- **Donald Bradley** - Collected Works of Donald Bradley - *Stock Market Prediction. Picking Winners. The Parallax Problem in Astrology. Solar & Lunar Returns. Profession & Birth Date. Taking the Kid Gloves off Astrology.* - (1950)
- **Sepharial (Walter Gorn Old)** - Sepharial's Arcana & Keys - *The Arcana of Stock & Share Key. Key to Sugar Values. Rubber. The Master Key. The Golden Key. The Eclipse System. The Solar Lunar Values. The Solar Apex Method.* - (1930)
- **J. Ross Tyler** - Financial Astrology - *The Key To Universal Law* - (1934)
- **Dr. Alexander Goulden** - Secrets of the Chronocrators - *An Advanced Course in Astrological Forecasting of Financial Markets* - (2014)
- **Dr. Alexander Goulden** - Behind the Veil - *Celestial Mechanics & Ancient Geometry in Financial Analysis* - (2010)
- **Daniele Prandelli** - The Law Of Cause And Effect - *Creating A Planetary Price/Time Map Of Market Action Through Sympathetic Resonance* - (2010)
- **T. G. Butaney, Financial Astrologer** - Forecasting Prices - *A Complete Course of Commercial Astrology* - (1940)
- **T. G. Butaney, Financial Astrologer** - How To Forecast Prices & Winners In Horse Races - *With Astrological Forecast Of Prices Or Cotton, Grains, Oil-Seeds & Rainfall* - (1947)
- **T. G. Butaney, Financial Astrologer** - Master Key Of Races - *All My Numerological & Astrological Secrets Discovered Over 30 Years' Experience* - (1970)
- **William D. Gann** - Collected Writings of W. D. Gann, Volume VI - *Astrological Writings* - (1955)
- **Muriel & Louis Hasbrouck** – Space Time Forecasting of Economic Trends – (1958-1006)
- **George Bayer** - Money Investing In Stocks, Trading In Commodities, Or The Time Factors In The Stock Market - *The Art of Scientifically Detecting Direction & Distance of Swings* - (1937)
- **George Bayer** - A Complete Course In Astrology - *Erection & Interpretation Of Horoscopes As Well As For Stocks* - (1937)
- **George Bayer** - Turning Four Hundred Years Of Astrology To Practical Use & Other Matters - (1944)
- **George Bayer** - Bible Interpretation - (1937)
- **Daniel T. Ferrera** - Studies In Astrological Bible Interpretation - (2001)

- **George J. McCormack** - Long-Range Astro-Weather Forecasting - *A Private, Comprehensive Technical Instruction Course* - (1965)
- **George J. McCormack** - ASTROTECH – *A Collection of Journals on Astrological Finance* - (1937-1941)
- **John Nelson** - Cosmic Patterns - (2006)
- **Thomas H. Graydon** - New Laws For Natural Phenomena - (1938)
- **W. T. Foster** - Sun Spots And Weather - (1907)
- **Cornelius Walford** - Famines Of The World - *Past & Present* - (1879)
- **Prof. Jos. Rodes Buchanan, M. D.** - Periodicity - *The Law Of All Life* - (1912)
- **Ray & Josephine Smythe** - Stars Ahead - (1942)
- **Sam Bartolet** - Eclipses & Lunations In Astrology - (1937)
- **Effie M. Cooley** - Astrological Relation Of Names & Numbers - (1912)
- **L. Edward Johndro** - Collected L. Edward Johndro - *The Stars, How And Where They Influence. The Earth in the Heavens. A New Concept of Sign Rulership. Astrological Dictionary & Self-Reading Horoscope* - (1927)
- **L. Edward Johndro** - Johndro's Collected Articles - 1930's - (1930)
- **Maurice Wemyss** - The Wheel Of Life Or Scientific Astrology - *5 Volumes Bound in 2 Hardcovers* - (1927)
- **Robert DeLuce** - Rectification Of The Horoscope - *Practical Lessons, Tables & Illustrations* - (1930)
- **Fred White** - A Guide To Astrology - *& Correcting The Time Of Birth* - (1901)
- **Gregorius** - The Master Key Of Destiny - (1924)
- **Paul Councel** - Your Stars And Destiny - (1940)
- **Mark Mellen** - How To Play The Races And Win - (1938)

www.ingramcontent.com/pod-product-compliance
Lightning Source LLC
LaVergne TN
LVHW081949200926
848484LV00009B/2532
9781942418108